SWIMMING

WITH

SHARKS

D1594468

SWIMMING

WITH

SHARKS

SURVIVING
NARCISSIST-INFESTED
WATERS

Alena Scigliano

BOOKLOGIX®
Alpharetta, Georgia

This publication is meant as a source of valuable information for the reader, however it is not meant as a substitute for direct expert assistance. If such a level of assistance is required, the services of a competent professional should be sought.

ISBN: 978-1-6653-0681-2 - Paperback
ISBN: 978-1-6653-0682-9 - Hardcover
eISBN: 978-1-6653-0683-6 - ePub
ISBN: 978-1-6653-0684-3 - Audiobook

These ISBNs are the property of BookLogix for the express purpose of sales and distribution of this title. The content of this book is the property of the copyright holder only. BookLogix does not hold any ownership of the content of this book and is not liable in any way for the materials contained within. The views and opinions expressed in this book are the property of the Author/Copyright holder, and do not necessarily reflect those of BookLogix.

Library of Congress Control Number: 2023912896

♾This paper meets the requirements of ANSI/NISO Z39.48-1992 (Permanence of Paper)

081623

For each person who was brave enough to seek counseling and kind enough to place their trust in me. You are the ones who gave me the knowledge and experience to be able to write this book and, in turn, help others. Your willingness to be vulnerable and your courage to say no to the narcissists in your lives is an inspiration to us all. You have been a precious part of my journey and my story, and you will forever be in my heart. Don't forget, you are each worthy just as you are. And for those of you who are just beginning this journey of soul-mending from narcissistic abuse, as long as you believe in yourself, no one can stop you.

CONTENTS

Preface   *ix*

Introduction   *xiii*

Prologue   *xix*

PART 1 – SHARK TALES

Chapter 1 – Sharks, Dolphins, and Narcissists   3

Chapter 2 – The Nature of Sharks and Narcissists   9

Chapter 3 – Fantasy vs. Reality   13

PART 2 – SWIMMING IN NARCISSIST-INFESTED WATERS

Chapter 4 – Shark Bites   21

Chapter 5 – Diving Deep into Narcissistic Abuse   25

Chapter 6 – Narcissistic Abuse Stress   39

Chapter 7 – Narcissistic Abuse Is Still Abuse   57

PART 3 – SURVIVING NARCISSIST-INFESTED WATERS

Chapter 8 – The Three Steps to Will Yourself
          Out of Narcissistic Abuse   65

Chapter 9 – Evaluating Your Options   69

Chapter 10 – Keeping Your Head Above Water:
       Handling Confrontations with Narcissists   77

Chapter 11 – Surviving the Hook   87

Chapter 12 – Prep Step 1: Resources   89

Chapter 13 – Prep Step 2: Legal Counsel   93

Chapter 14 – Prep Step 3: Documentation   97

Chapter 15 – Prep Step 4: Self-Care   103

Chapter 16 – Parenting Alongside a Narcissist   109

PART 4 – THE NATURE OF NARCISSISTS

Chapter 17 – What is Empathy?   121

Chapter 18 – What Is a Narcissist?   125

Chapter 19 – Shark Species: Types of Narcissists   141

Chapter 20 – The Narcissist's Inner World   147

Chapter 21 – Narcissists and Shame   153

Chapter 22 – Narcissists and Power   157

Chapter 23 – Narcissistic Supply   161

Chapter 24 – Narcissistic Parents   165

Chapter 25 – Other Narcissists in Our Lives   171

PART 5 – NAVIGATING FORWARD

Chapter 26 – The Seven Stages of Soul-Mending   181

Chapter 27 – Empowering Knowledge   193

Chapter 28 – Jumping Back In   201

Shark Detector   209

Epilogue   223

Acknowledgments   231

PREFACE
OR
WHAT TO EXPECT
OR
WHY'D YOU PUT *THAT* IN THERE, ALENA?

I f you've already read every other book out there about narcissism and narcissistic abuse, don't worry, this won't be more of just the same. *Swimming with Sharks: Surviving Narcissist-Infested Waters* materialized from a combination of my clinical experience as a Licensed Professional Counselor and psychotherapist, the theories, concepts, and ways of explaining pathological narcissism that I've developed as an innovative thinker, and the inspiration we all can access but don't always pay attention to. In other words, it's full of unique ideas and inspiring messages you won't find anywhere else. I've specialized in narcissistic abuse for most of my career, and providing therapy is fulfilling and rewarding. However, spending an hour with each individual means that I can only help a few at a time. My hope is that this book makes it possible for many more people to benefit from what I've learned as a healer.

"Swimming with Sharks Growth Book"

Don't miss this companion to *Swimming with Sharks*. It is full of great material to help you process some of the deeper aspects of the book and how you've been impacted by narcissistic abuse as well as material to support you on this journey. One of my favorite parts is definitely the "Shareables for Friends & Family" section—an assortment of handouts I created that you can provide to the people you'll need as part of your support system while dealing with the narcissist in your life.

Throughout *Swimming with Sharks***, you'll come across "Growth Moments" that look like this . . .**

 Growth Moment

If you have the companion guide to this book, the *Swimming with Sharks Growth Book*, take a moment here to check out the _____.

Sometimes, the Growth Moments will give you journaling or reflection suggestions, and other times they will refer you to the supplemental material provided in the *Growth Book*. If you don't have the *Swimming with Sharks Growth Book* yet, I invite you to check it out on my website, www.AlenaScigliano.com, or find it at your favorite book retailer.

*****Side Note:** While the *Growth Book* functions somewhat like a workbook, I am highly averse to the idea of doing workbooks but love the idea of therapeutic growth. Even in my private group practice, I request that each of the therapists use the term, "between-session growth activity," rather than, "homework." I'm pretty sure we were all at least a little traumatized by the relentless onslaught of homework throughout our academic years, so I don't think it's super effective to trigger the negative feelings some of us might have in reaction to the inclusion of "workbook" in the title. So, please don't think of the companion *Growth Book* as work—it truly is meant to be an easy way to support you in your growth beyond the hurt caused by narcissistic abuse.

Why So Colorful?

Pathological narcissism and narcissistic abuse can feel like dry and cold topics to discuss, not to mention overwhelming and hopeless at times. Those who are in the midst of a narcissistic relationship, healing during the aftermath of one, or anywhere in between, are typically in a state of distress, often resembling that of PTSD. Furthermore, your life is busy and packed with obligations. You don't have time to sit and become absorbed in dense material. I wanted to share this book in a less overwhelming format. That is why you will find bright colors and graphics throughout, rather than visually dense content. I hope it is one tiny way that I can make your journey a little bit easier.

Use of Analogies

The most effective teachers teach something new while connecting it to something already known, so analogies are one of the most effective ways to learn new material. I love to use analogies in my work, and over the years, I've tried to keep track of those I've come up with during sessions. You'll find many of these sprinkled throughout the book. Some may speak to you and some may not. Overall though, I hope they help you move forward in your growth journey.

Relationship & Gender Inclusiveness

In addition to romantic relationships with narcissists, *Swimming with Sharks* is for people who find themselves involved in any sort of relationship with a narcissist, as well as those within the healing community who work with victims of narcissistic abuse or narcissists themselves. The concepts you find here will apply to any relationship, whether that is with a partner, an ex-partner, a parent, a child, a friend, a coworker, a boss, a pastor, a neighbor, or anyone else in your life who might be a narcissist. Oftentimes, when people come to see me regarding a narcissistic partner, we also discover that one of their parents was or is a narcissist. Alternatively, I've had many patients come to me solely because they believe that one of their parents is a narcissist, not because they are experiencing any abuse in their partnerships. Narcissistic behaviors are generally consistent across the board, so even if the entirety of this book does not apply to you, you will most certainly find value in seeing the information through the lens of other relationships.

With the hope that the material will feel applicable to any reader, I have tried to use language that is not only relationship-neutral but also gender-neutral. Not every narcissistic partner is a man, not every narcissistic parent is a woman, and not every narcissist or reader theirself will identify with a binary gender assignment. *Swimming with Sharks* is inclusive of any gender assignment and respectful of all gender pronoun choices. With that in mind, when you come across the word "theirself," it is not a typo. Grammatically, it makes far more sense to use this in conjunction with the singular and gender-neutral "they" than the word "themselves."

INTRODUCTION
NOT
"SKIP THIS TO GET TO THE GOOD STUFF"

~

THE *GOOD* STUFF ALREADY STARTED!

S *wimming with Sharks* teaches you fundamental aspects of pathological narcissism and narcissistic abuse that are essential to understanding, surviving, and soul-mending from any type of relationship with a narcissist. Whether you choose to stay in your relationship with a narcissist or leave (or stay in contact or "go no contact"), this book will guide you in breaking free of the chains any narcissist has clasped on you in order to maintain control over you. It will teach you how to take back that control. Narcissists can strip away hope, bit by bit. I want to help you rediscover your hope and strength to be able to draw upon even when you are face-to-face with the monstrous side of a narcissist. You may not always believe it, but you will be able to find strength within yourself to break free of any chains that bind you.

Your Guide Map to the Book

You may notice that the content in *Swimming with Sharks* is organized differently than you would typically find in this type of book. I've prioritized the information that will help you understand your own experience to come before that which will help you understand narcissists themselves. Depending on where you are on your journey though, you may find it helpful to jump around to different parts of the book. Here are some quick suggestions:

If you are curious about the messaging behind the shark analogy, or if you are a lover of fairy tales, start from the beginning with "Mermaid and the Shark" in the Prologue and continue reading through Part One.

If you are just beginning your journey of understanding narcissistic abuse, you may want to jump straight to Part Two, to shore up your foundational knowledge on the subject. Even if you have already done your research, though, make sure you don't miss this part. It includes some original concepts I'm introducing, such as Narcissistic Abuse Stress and Narcissistic Abuse Stress Disorder.

If you are actively in a relationship with a narcissist and would like to explore options regarding what to do next, then Part Three will be your go-to section.

For those readers who would like to gain a deeper understanding of the nature of narcissists and pathological narcissism, then Part Four will take you on a deep dive into that realm.

On the other hand, if you are no longer in the relationship and are ready to figure out how to move forward and toward soul-mending, then you'll want to check out Part Five. This is where you will also find the Shark Detector—a guide on how to avoid ending up in a relationship with another narcissist.

"Victim" or "Survivor"?

Victim or survivor? Which word do you prefer? There's been some debate in my world over these words. Some disagree with the use of the word "victim" out of concern that those who are victimized by narcissists will take it on as their identity and feel like something is wrong with them, instead of accurately recognizing that the problem lies in the narcissist. On the other hand, while you're still stuck with a narcissist, it's hard to feel like you're a survivor. Let's face it, if someone's leg is still clenched in the jaws of a shark, they're still a victim of that shark attack. That doesn't mean that being a victim becomes their whole identity. But at that moment, you better believe they're going to be feeling like a victim.

I completely understand that in situations such as having cancer, identifying oneself as a victim has many negative implications and can actually be a hindrance to healing. The thing is, you can't walk out on cancer, but you can walk out on a narcissist. And rarely does someone choose to walk out on a narcissist if they haven't acknowledged that they are the victim of narcissistic abuse.

In the years that I've been working with narcissistic abuse, I commonly witness a resistance in my patients to acknowledge that they are being abused. Some are shocked that I would even use the word abuse. Others refuse to verbalize the word themselves. Until you are honest with yourself, though, and accept that you are in fact being abused, you are far less likely to make the necessary changes in your life to stop the abuse.

I had been using the word "victim" in all of my writings, but when a colleague I greatly respect stated that she doesn't like to use that word, I started to question myself. I did my best to find a substitute. I considered switching to "survivor," as she uses, or potentially "target." That same day, though, my husband was talking to me about the carnal news footage he had seen of the Russian invasion of Ukraine. He described the videos and photos that were shown on European news networks but not on the news in the United States. Photos of children who had been killed, lying in the streets with their mothers crying over them. Pregnant women, dead, after a maternity ward was struck by a missile.

Can you imagine how unempathic it would be to tell a grieving mother that her child was a target, rather than a victim? None of these people were targets in this war. They were victims. And the dead children and mothers certainly weren't survivors. I also imagine that the ones still living feel more like victims than survivors, in fact, many of them will likely experience survivor's guilt. Furthermore, the fact that the European public was being exposed to the realities of the war meant that they were becoming outraged and calling for change. Protecting American citizens from disturbing images means that they don't see the whole picture and they don't readily cry out for change. Being exposed to the truth of an atrocity is an important part of motivating society to make change happen.

Narcissistic abuse is an atrocity too. Not only is pathological narcissism one of the underlying causes of wars, it causes immense destruction within families and communities everywhere. And not everyone survives. There are children, families, and others who are murdered by narcissistic parents, even after the other parent warns the court of the danger and begs it to protect their children. These people are not survivors of narcissistic abuse. They were victims.

It was during the conversation with my husband that something clicked. I was reminded of the analogy I use that describes being narcissistically abused as similar to being in a war, only the rest of the world can't see your wounds. Thinking about that, while also having the reality of war unfolding in real time, I realized that I **need** to use the word "victim." There is no other word that does justice to how it feels to be on the receiving end of narcissistic abuse. More so than that, I believe that there is actually power in the word victim—power to incite change.

I want to not only help individuals put a stop to being abused, I want to help empower society as a whole to put a stop to the ongoing narcissistic abuse that occurs throughout all of society—from families, to churches, to corporations, to the government. If we want the world to truly change, we have to address the presence of pathological narcissism and narcissistic abuse. Until the world opens its eyes to the fact that millions of people are victims of narcissistic abuse, no one is going to try to change how things work. So if we want to really incite change in individuals and in society, we need to bravely own the label "victim."

With the above points taken into consideration, I was inspired to use both terms at the same time because they both apply. Now, I use the term "survivor-victim," and I think it works quite well to capture the state of anyone who was or is currently in a relationship with a narcissist.

While you are considering whether or not to use "survivor," "victim," or "survivor-victim," one thing to keep in mind is to respect what someone wants to be called. If your friend really wants to be referred to as a narcissistic abuse survivor, then don't slap the word victim in their face—call them a survivor.

If you are a therapist and working with this population, discern what is therapeutically appropriate at any given moment. There are times when I've needed to use the word "victim" with a patient in order to help them move into the contemplation stage of change. Other times, I choose "survivor" because I know that they need encouragement and to hear me validate the hard work they've been doing to set up boundaries. Recently, "survivor-victim" has typically been the most appropriate term, but use your therapeutic intuition to discern which term you use and when. If you aren't sure, ask your patient. If you make a mistake, apologize and process it with them.

Ultimately, we need to remember that being a victim of someone else's abusive behaviors does not define who we are. We get to decide who we are and who we want to be—no one else. So when you come across the word "victim" in this book, remember that I'm using that term to help motivate change. Most importantly, never forget that while you may be a victim right now, you have the power to turn yourself into a survivor-victim and even a survivor.

I know things got a little heavy in the discussion over survivor vs. victim. I promise that the rest of the book does not bear that same level of intensity, at least not intentionally. I hope reading this book will help you to make sense of the situation in which you find yourself, determine what **you** believe you need to do, and give you a little extra hope and strength. Whether you choose to maintain your relationship with a narcissist or move toward independent recovery, I am confident that *Swimming with Sharks* will inspire you to make meaningful change in your life.

🦈 **Growth Moment**

If you have the companion guide to this book, the *Swimming with Sharks Growth Book*, take a moment here to check out the *Survivor, Victim, or Survivor-Victim* reflection page.

PROLOGUE

OR

STORY TIME

Mermaid and the Shark

O nce upon a time, there were kingdoms deep under the sea, just as there were on land. Into one of these kingdoms and up to the castle did a young sea witch wander one stormy night as the currents thrashed her about. She knocked on the door and begged the young merprince for shelter, but his cold and unfeeling heart turned her away. After the door slammed shut, she turned around, and, tossing off her cloak of sea kelp, a beautiful glow began to emanate from within her. The glow was so bright and beautiful that the prince turned back to open the door, then beckoned her to enter and take shelter. However, it was too late. The sea witch had already witnessed what was truly in his heart. She pulled out her coral staff and struck the ocean floor with it. Rippling outward, her spell overtook the castle and its inhabitants, turning what was once a beautiful coral reef filled with every color of the spectrum and bleaching it white and dead. Along with the castle and every other creature within it undergoing a metamorphosis, the prince transformed into a hideous hammerhead shark, covered in what appeared to be long-ago healed wounds to represent the scars on his heart.

Trapped in his lost kingdom, the shark could only wallow in his misery, alone, until one day, a sweet, innocent, and beautiful mermaid happened upon the castle of dead coral after falling off and losing her seahorse in the midst of being chased by bull sharks. As she entered the unlocked door of the castle, she was struck by how cold the water felt inside. Something didn't feel quite right. Welcomed by some friendly, if not scary-looking crustaceans, she found herself whisked away to a room where she could rest. Later, she was introduced to the hammerhead shark at dinner. Despite his ghastly appearance at first glance, he was quite charming. They laughed and shared stories throughout the dinner, and he asked her to dance after dessert. The beautiful mermaid was swept away by his enchantment. She fell asleep that night, peacefully. Feeling safer than she ever had before, she dreamt of what wonders lay ahead for her future.

The mermaid spent every day in the company of the shark. No longer noticing his scars, she only saw his charm. As she grew more and more attached though, and he grew more and more secure in that attachment, she saw glimpses of his shark-like nature creep out. Flashes of anger and rage would appear like fireworks but then disappear just as quickly, leaving a trail of wonder and disbelief in the mermaid's mind. When she would ask the shark about his sudden mood shifts, he was dismissive, telling her that she must be imagining things and that he never behaved in those ways. Eventually, she began to question her reality, unsure of what had really happened and what hadn't. So she reassured herself that she must have been overreacting.

As time passed though, the shark became more aggressive in his verbal attacks, more contemptuous toward the mermaid, and more antagonistic. The underwater castle began to feel cold and lonely once again. The mermaid had isolated herself from her friends and family, hoping to avoid them becoming aware of the shark's behavior toward her. She thought that they wouldn't understand him or why he treated her the way he did. The mermaid believed that it came from the abuses of his past and that if she showed him enough love, he would eventually turn back into the charming shark he had been when they first met. Day after day, she held onto the hope that he would change. After all, he frequently promised that he would, sharing with her the beautiful visions he had for their future. Blinded by his manipulation, the mermaid repeatedly excused the shark's selfish and tyrannical behavior, sometimes even telling herself that his controlling behavior meant that he truly loved her. If he didn't love her, then he wouldn't care about what she did. The justifications were numerous, and as each new day began, she would forget about the toxicity from the day before.

To be continued . . .

Part One

SHARK TALES

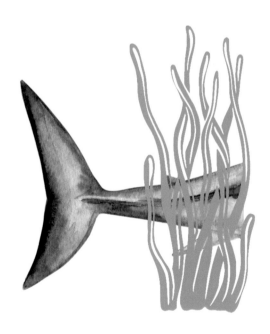

Chapter 1

SHARKS, DOLPHINS, AND NARCISSISTS

Who doesn't love a good dolphin tale? *Flipper*—the show and the movie; *Free Willy* (Yes, Orcas, a.k.a. Killer Whales, are the largest species of dolphin); even *Shark Tale*, the animated favorite in which a shark masquerades itself as a dolphin, are all stories in which we find dolphins to be irresistible. Their intelligence is considered by many scientists to be second only to humans. Their grace and aerobatics enchant us at aquariums, and we're mesmerized watching them breach the ocean's surface offshore. They are playful and adorable as puppies yet as powerful as lions. Courageous protectors in the sea, dolphins have been known to fight off sharks on behalf of other species, including humans. Even vacationers to Florida and the Caribbean don't hesitate to let their young children swim with dolphins. It's almost as if we have an inherent trust in the species to not harm us.

So how does this relate to sharks and narcissists? Much like dolphins, narcissists can be enchanting at first glance. Their charm, charisma, cleverness, and intelligence draw you in, while their playfulness, loving behavior, and wit keep you wanting more. You feel safe and secure with them. And when their attention is focused on you, you can't help but feel privileged. Out of everyone else, this amazing creature has chosen you to be the object of their attention. Because you've been drawn into their appeal, your brain assumes that this person is harmless and safe, similar to how we think of dolphins.

It's like taking a glance at a sign and reading one thing when it says another. Our brains are wired to make assumptions based on past knowledge, combined with the current context, to quickly make a determination regarding safety. The problem is, our brains sometimes get it wrong. They can misinterpret the cues our eyes perceive and make incorrect assumptions. So when you first meet a narcissist, you don't realize they're a narcissist. There are likely early warning signs that they aren't as innocent as they seem, but your brain doesn't pick up on those cues, or if it does, it disregards them or rationalizes them. In other words, your brain interprets the narcissist to be a dolphin, rather than the more accurate conclusion—a shark.

Let me demonstrate the connection between each of these concepts by describing how this type of scenario might occur if you were really out in the ocean. Imagine being out on a boat with friends on a hot summer day in search of dolphins. You decide to cool off by taking a quick dip in the water. As you're swimming next to the boat, you see a fin pop above the surface. Since you were specifically looking for dolphins, your brain automatically interprets what you are seeing as the fin of a dolphin. and you are filled with excitement at the idea of swimming close to one. Shrieking with joy, you call out to your friends on the boat to look. The fin disappears below the surface, and when it pops back up again, you try to swim closer, secretly imagining it letting you hold on, pulling you through the water, just like you've seen in the movies.

Noticing the fin cutting through the water in your direction, you think your dreams are coming true. Once it gets close though, the animal begins to behave a little more aggressively than you had anticipated. You feel the snout nudge you under the water and recognize the pain that precedes a bruise on your flesh. Confusion sets in because this isn't what you expected, but you tell yourself it's nothing and that the dolphin is just trying to play with you. Soon after though, the aggressive behavior escalates. You feel a slash across your thigh, unsure of where it came from. Stunned, you stay where you are, treading water and trying to assess what is happening. Without further warning, you glimpse a set of jaws opening up in the water below and latching onto your leg but then quickly letting go. Rather than fight or flight, your freeze instinct remains. Finally, fear forces you to start considering that perhaps you weren't swimming with a dolphin at all. Now that the pain is setting in, it's certainly starting to feel like this must be a shark.

In a real-life scenario, your friends would be screaming at you to climb back into the boat, and most people would listen. Knowing how dangerous sharks are, their survival instinct would take over and automatically lead them to safety.

When it comes to

relationships with narcissists though, that's not at all what happens. The parallel would be staying in the water even though you've been hurt, trying to convince yourself that the creature in the water with you is just a dolphin. You might say something to yourself like,

> "It was just trying to catch a fish and accidentally grazed my side. It didn't mean to hurt me."

Even though you've noticed your wounds, you continue to make excuses and rationalize the animal's behavior,

> "I know that deep down it really is a dolphin and must really love me, otherwise, it would have swam away by now."

For some reason, that feels safer than seeing it for what it is, a shark, and then scrambling out of the water. You might even go so far as to claim,

> "But I'm tired of waiting around for the perfect dolphin to show up. I know the shark isn't perfect, but if I can just hold out long enough, maybe it will start acting like a dolphin."

Amid your lingering uncertainty, another bite is taken out of your side, and your mind is once again reminded that the figure in the water is a shark. Eventually, the back-and-forth thoughts may cause you to start questioning your sanity. Trying to make sense of the situation, you might even start to question whether or not you are actually the one who is a shark. Desperate to regain any sense of control, you are willing to consider even the most implausible of ideas.

Clarity sets in though with the next attack. With no arteries severed, it's not enough to kill you, but it is just enough to cause the type of pain that makes you too afraid to swim away now. You worry that if you do, that will be the point at which you won't survive. Your eyes see what's lurking in the water, and you finally acknowledge that you have indeed been swimming with a shark all along—all illusions of dolphins have vanished. You have no idea how to escape, though. With less and less energy, you find yourself struggling to keep your head above water. Sometimes, it might even feel like it would be easier to just give in and sink to the bottom.

If you've ever been in a relationship with a narcissist, the scenario above won't seem as outlandish to you as it might to others. This is a realistic analogy to what happens within narcissistically abusive relationships. Unfortunately, we don't see how dangerous the situation is when we're talking about humans rather than sharks. It wasn't the animal turning out to be a shark that created the greatest danger in this story. It was holding out for the animal to be the dolphin we were hoping it was, despite all warning signs pointing to it being a shark, that caused the real danger. Sharks are inevitably present in the ocean, but once we notice their presence, we don't have to stay in the water with them.

Chapter 2

THE NATURE OF SHARKS AND NARCISSISTS

While *Jaws* was a blockbuster hit and became a cult classic, it also led to incredible damage to the ecosystem. Preying upon fear for artistic value had the unanticipated side effect of leading to ignorant misconceptions of the real dangers, or lack thereof, of sharks. This resulted in a shameful decimation of sharks and a vital species to our ecosystem. People overreacted, as they often do, and acted to an extreme. As with anything, we must process information within an educated context. Sharks are not swimming up to our beaches on the hunt for humans. When shark attacks occur, it is not because sharks have a psychopathic desire for human flesh. They simply get hungry like the rest of us, search for food, and opportunistically and instinctively eat when something is moving in the water. It is their nature to eat, and the traits with which they were born make them powerful and sometimes scary.

Similarly, narcissists are not prowling our metaphorical waters hunting you down. They are opportunistic, and they are hungry. Their nature is to latch onto anyone who supplies them with sustenance, also known as narcissistic supply. If they come across someone who doesn't provide what they're looking for, they move on. But when they happen upon an empathic nurturer, they can't help but gravitate toward and latch onto the empath for the nourishment they provide. Empaths make narcissists feel good about themselves. Who wouldn't want to stick around for more of that?

I want to make it crystal clear that I am not trying to demonize sharks OR narcissists. Nor am I trying to engender fear of narcissists. Every narcissist is someone's child, someone's friend, someone's lover or partner, possibly someone's parent, and according to my faith, a child of our creator. They are still human and deserving of love and acceptance. But just like we can appreciate or, dare I say, love a shark, we know to do it from afar if we want to keep ourselves safe because we've accepted sharks for what they are. Sharks are powerful creatures that we can respect. We can respect narcissists in the same way, but unfortunately, narcissists and mutual respect do not coexist. Respecting ourselves means being intolerant of anyone abusing us. The best way to do that is to maintain our distance, just like we do with sharks.

My guess is that if you're reading this book right now, the idea of maintaining your distance from your narcissist is currently improbable, impossible, or unfathomable. That's okay! I am not going to spend the rest of this book trying to *convince* you to swim away, end a relationship, go "no contact," or anything similar. I know that is unrealistic for most people and unfair to put that pressure on you. Creating distance from a narcissist is a life-altering choice that usually impacts many innocent people. It will never be an easy decision. In fact, part of this book is written for those who choose to keep the narcissist in their life and how to do it in as healthy a way as possible. For now, all I want to do is help you begin to change how you conceptualize your narcissist by thinking of them as you do a shark, with acceptance of their nature by not expecting them to change.

We don't expect sharks to change their nature, so why do we hope narcissists will change theirs?

Chapter 3

FANTASY VS. REALITY

Many people wonder what makes them so vulnerable to narcissists. Why is it so easy for them to fall into a relationship with a narcissist and then feel like they can't get out? While the answer to this is very nuanced and comes in many different layers—which will be addressed throughout this book—I wanted to first share a theory I have developed. It addresses a major problem I've noticed in society. We have a pattern of holding onto fantasy, rather than accepting reality, to the detriment of ourselves and those around us, including our children.

Fairy Tales

Disney's *Beauty and the Beast* came out when I was a little girl, and Belle's character strongly resonated with me. She was smart and courageous, as well as forgiving and full of grace. She embodied strength along with empathy, and her love was so powerful that a single tear could transform a beast into a prince.

I recall desperately wanting Belle's yellow ball gown to wear as my Halloween costume. I saw it in a costume shop one time, and it was the most gorgeous dress my young eyes had ever seen. I wanted to look as beautiful as Belle did in her ballgown because, even as a child, I was lured into the appeal of the romance that her dress represented. I'm sure that on some subconscious level, I was hoping that my prince would show up during trick-or-treating to whisk me off into a waltz.

While the story of *Beauty and the Beast* is beautiful, it can also be a dangerous tale. From a very young age, we receive message after message, teaching us that our love can transform anyone. Society, through the use of fairy tales and other media, convinces us to believe that if we hang in there and provide enough love for long enough, any beast can be reformed into a prince(ss/x) charming.

If you pay close attention to the beginning of *Beauty and the Beast* though, you'll notice that there was a reason the witch turned the prince into a beast in the first place. The prince was an entitled, arrogant, and unempathic narcissist, a beast in human form and definitely not Prince Charming. Once becoming a literal beast, the prince has only one requirement to return to his human self—find a woman who will fall in love with him. While his manners are certainly beastly in the beginning, we are witness to Belle's persistent work in turning the beast into a gentleman. Once he begins to treat her kindly, she slowly begins to fall in love. His transformation culminates in a metamorphosis back to his human state, at which point he is portrayed as the iconic Prince Charming—a perfect and loving match for Belle. The lasting moral of the story: Through Belle's consistent attention, coaching, and love, the arrogant and disdainful prince he once was seemingly disappeared.

"Mermaid and the Shark" Reflections

I'm sure you noticed the parallels between *Mermaid and the Shark* and *Beauty and the Beast*, especially at the beginning. My version of the classic tale, however, is far more realistic and representative of what happens in real life. We don't know exactly how much time passed while the mermaid was in her narcissistic relationship. Purposefully, this is to demonstrate that regardless of the amount of time spent in a narcissistically abusive relationship, the impact is detrimental to the healthy functioning of the victim, and the recovery can take years.

The sea witch was able to see through the merman's facade. Had the mermaid been able to identify early on that the shark was a narcissist, she would have simply accepted him for the shark that he was without trying to change him into the prince she thought he could be. Imagine how much time and heartache she would have saved had this been her experience. Most likely, she would have left after the second or third time he treated her abusively because she wouldn't have had false hope or felt an obligation to stick around and wait for change that never came.

The Fairy Tale Paradigm

In the real world, Belle's love would never have the power to transform the beast, just as the mermaid couldn't change the shark. He would most certainly remain a cruel beast for the rest of his life because that is what he always was. Unfortunately, we've been convinced that fairy tales can be reality. Believing that lie, we live our lives and make choices in our relationships based on false hope. Brainwashed through books, film, and even the messages we receive from our caregivers, we believe we have the power to transform someone who treats us in unacceptable and abusive ways into a loving, kind, and empathic partner. As I'm sure you are starting to see, this isn't reflective of real life.

If you've done previous research on narcissists or narcissistic abuse, you may have noticed the term "prince charming" being used when describing how a narcissist behaves at the very beginning of a relationship. Because we've been brainwashed by the fairy tale concept and are vulnerable to false hope, using that term makes it seem like a prince charming was inside our narcissist to begin with, and it could inadvertently perpetuate the notion that the abusive version of a narcissist can be changed *back* into a prince charming. Instead, we need to dispel the myth that there ever was a prince charming by changing the paradigm.

> **🐟 Growth Moment**
>
> If you have the companion guide to this book, the *Swimming with Sharks Growth Book*, take a moment here to check out the *Your Fairy Tale* activity.

The Shark Tale Paradigm

If you were to go swimming in the ocean and see a shark nearby, you would most certainly make a mad dash out of the water. You wouldn't hang around, waiting to see if it's a nice shark. Nope, you know exactly what a shark is. You learned about the danger of sharks as a child, and you've carried that knowledge throughout adulthood, keeping an eye out for telltale signs every time you go to the beach. Remember the story earlier about the dolphin that turned out to be a shark? If you had just seen the shark for what it was the moment it first bumped into you, you would have immediately exited the water with only bruises to tell the story.

When it comes to narcissists, we need to start thinking of them as sharks. This is what I call the Shark Tale Paradigm.

We must shift to believing this over the fairy tale. Once we can do this, victims will be more likely to leave their narcissistically abusive relationships early on and before they become too deeply invested. This new way of conceptualizing narcissists as being no different than sharks will liberate victims from believing they are obligated to stay in a narcissistic relationship.

Next, you'll read the conclusion of *Mermaid and the Shark*. As opposed to the conclusion of *Beauty and the Beast*, this story ends

with the Shark Tale Paradigm in mind, providing a more realistic picture of the nature of the narcissistic shark and a healthier depiction of the mermaid's response.

Mermaid and the Shark

Conclusion

Finding no relief, the mermaid's delusional hope eventually gave way to despair, depression, and a feeling of helplessness. She felt trapped and imprisoned until in a moment of enlightenment, she realized that the bars on her prison cell were in her mind. Something shifted, and she knew that she had never deserved to be treated like this. She finally saw the shark's behavior for what it was—abuse. And not only that, she accepted that he would never change and that she had no control over getting him to change. In her heart, she knew that there would never be a magical transformation to turn him back into a merprince, for it was only the outside that had been changed by the sea witch. His character had always been that way. Even though she felt afraid and ashamed, she reached out to her friends and family for support. With their help and encouragement, she gathered the strength and courage to swim out of the bleached coral castle and never look back.

Transitioning to a new life wasn't easy. For a long time, the shark reached out to her and begged her to return to him. He sent her bouquets of sea anemones with cards that promised her the world. He told her how much he loved her and how he couldn't live without her. Even though it took all the strength she could muster, the mermaid managed to maintain the strict boundaries she had set and ignored his attempts to draw her back in. At some point, the shark must have realized that he wasn't going to succeed in winning her back because he finally stopped contacting her.

Fearful, the mermaid eventually tried dating again. She met another merperson who was kind and loving toward her all the time, not just when they wanted something. While the mermaid had to work through the after-effects of the trauma she had endured, her new partner supported her through it all. One day, she found out that the abuse she experienced had a specific name—narcissistic abuse. Today, she finds purpose in educating others about the dangers of narcissistic abuse, how to identify it, how to break free from it, and how to move on. Healed for the most part now, with only

faint scars of memories to tell the tale, the mermaid is living her best life, full of the joy, love, and healthy companionship she had always dreamt she'd have.

🐚 Growth Moment

If you have the companion guide to this book, the *Swimming with Sharks Growth Book*, take a moment here to check out the *Your Shark Tale* activity.

Part Two

SWIMMING IN
NARCISSIST-INFESTED
WATERS

*Narcissistic Abuse
and the Damage it Causes*

Chapter 4

SHARK BITES

On the rare occasion that a shark bites a human, once they get a taste, the shark releases them because humans don't taste right to them. Unfortunately, because we instinctively struggle to get away once bitten, the damage our body sustains ends up being much worse than if we had just allowed the shark to let us go. Similarly, narcissists often move from person to person, because they don't find what they're looking for. If one person doesn't taste quite right, they'll move on to someone else. Struggling against the shark is what leaves those bitten by sharks more deeply wounded and is often the reason shark attacks turn fatal. Similarly, we are often hurt worse by narcissists because of our instinct to struggle rather than allowing the narcissist to just move on.

As you may have experienced as an adult, it's not nearly as easy to find and build lasting close friendships as it was when we were children. A few years ago, my husband and I became friends with another couple. We were so excited to finally have friends who not only had kids the same ages as ours but were also fun to be around. They showed interest in us and our lives while openly sharing their lives with us as well. We spent a lot of time together and thought we were growing a friendship that would last a lifetime.

Unfortunately, about nine months into the friendship, something shifted with them. They started ghosting us after saying they would stop by to hang out. We began noticing an increasing number of gatherings to which we were no longer invited. We'd happen upon them at the beach with other people, the same people they once invited us to join. We felt rejected and hurt, not understanding what happened and why everything changed all of a sudden. Confused, we tried our best to make sense of it. I blamed myself, thinking that I must have offended them (I can be a little outspoken, so it wouldn't have been the first time). My husband attempted to rationalize what happened in other ways. Finally, though, we started putting the pieces together. Stepping back to objectively observe what was going on, we noticed a pattern. The people they were focusing more attention on were people who could give them something or make them feel special. Our specialness had worn off. Armed with this knowledge, we concluded that as a couple, they were functioning as a pathological narcissist does.

Just like how a shark takes a bite of something and then moves on once they realize they don't like the taste of it, our friends took a bite of us and eventually decided they didn't like how we tasted either. When they realized that we were no longer going to serve as a source of narcissistic supply[1] to them, they dropped us and moved on to the next possible prey. Seriously, we watched it happen. And sure enough, once they got what they wanted from the family after us, we noticed that they were no longer spending time with them either. Presumably, they moved on once again.

---

[1] See Chapter 23 - Narcissistic Supply

What our friends didn't take into consideration when they fostered our relationship but then dismissed us like we were never friends to begin with was the damage that they would cause as a result. My husband and I were deeply hurt, and it took a very long time for that wound to heal. We spent much more time mourning the loss of our friends than the amount of time the relationship actually lasted. And if I'm being honest, the wound still hasn't completely healed for either one of us. But what I have learned from the experience is that we would have been far less hurt had we not struggled to hold onto the relationship and instead allowed our fantasy of what could have been to fade as quickly as they swam away.

Chapter 5

DIVING DEEP INTO
NARCISSISTIC ABUSE

Narcissistic abuse describes a pattern of ongoing psychological abuse that occurs within relationships where at least one person exhibits pathological levels of narcissistic and antagonistic personality traits. At their core, narcissists are deeply insecure and have a very fragile self-image. Because narcissists were never taught healthy coping skills, they don't know how to heal their insecurities. Their perpetual insecurity and fragile self-worth make them vulnerable to shame. As with all humans, feeling vulnerable leads to an underlying fear. And how are we wired to handle fear? We try to take control. One way narcissists try to take control is by using others to make them feel good about theirselves. Unfortunately, because narcissists have not been taught healthy interpersonal relationship skills, they inevitably hurt those who are closest to them by treating them in dysfunctional and psychologically abusive ways, which is what we call Narcissistic Abuse. My chosen abbreviation is NAb, which you will see interchangeably used with the full term throughout the book.

NAb can occur either by sheer accident or because of self-interest. What many people don't realize is that most narcissists don't intend to hurt you. Your typical pathological narcissist doesn't *want* to do harm. They do harm without realizing it. Think of it like this. It's much like standing on someone's shoulders to be able to reach high enough to climb over a wall. When your heel digs into their shoulder, the infliction of pain is accidental—an unanticipated side effect of your need to be hoisted high enough to reach the top of the wall. In terms of what a narcissist does, the act of climbing over the wall represents their attempt at surviving their emotional insecurity and avoiding shattering their fragile self-image. The fear of facing their insecurities and the risk of crushing their self-image prevents them from having the insight to be able to anticipate the pain they will cause. Additionally, once they realize they've inflicted pain, the very nature of being insecure prevents them from acknowledging what they've done, much less apologizing for it. Rather than saying, "I'm so sorry that my heels hurt your shoulders, but thank you for helping me out," they might say, "I didn't hurt you. My heels didn't even touch your shoulders. I was standing on the balls of my feet. If your shoulders hurt, that's probably because you were holding me wrong."

Now, all of this is not to say that you won't come across pathological narcissists who clearly seem to be purposeful in their harm to others. You may even be in a relationship like this. The ones who want to do harm, though, are far rarer and specifically have sociopathic tendencies. This will be discussed later in the book when we explore the various "shark species," or types of narcissists.

One phenomenon inherent to having a relationship with a narcissist is typically not realizing that the way in which you are being treated is not only unhealthy and unacceptable but is in fact abusive. Whether you are just now realizing it or have known for a long time that your partner, ex-partner, parent, sibling, friend, coworker, pastor, or anyone else in your life is a narcissist, you do not have to sacrifice being treated with kindness as part of maintaining a relationship with someone. What helps is being able to identify what are and what aren't narcissistically abusive behaviors. In the following sections, we'll review the most common traits and tactics of abusive narcissists to better understand how we are hurt by them.

Traits of Pathological Narcissists

Being able to articulate what you have experienced within an antagonistic relationship is an important tool that will help you express yourself to others as well as move forward on your journey toward soul-mending. One way to make this easier is to improve your narcissistic traits vocabulary. I've included two lists of terms below. One is an abbreviated list of the terms that are most commonly used to describe pathological narcissists. Just in case those terms don't fully describe the narcissist you know, the second list is a much longer catalog of terms that could potentially apply. I have only included words that I have known to be applicable at one time or another. Many of these terms are synonyms; however, in case one resonates more than another, I wanted to include as many options as possible.

As you will see, some of these characteristics can be found in each of us at one time or another. The distinguishing factor between how a narcissist displays these traits and how the rest of us do is the longevity or severity to which they are present. No narcissist will possess each of these, so please don't make the mistake of thinking that someone has to hold all of the traits to behave as a pathological narcissist.

Core List of Traits of Pathological Narcissists

- ☐ Angry
- ☐ Angry Disagreeable
- ☐ Antagonistic
- ☐ Argumentative
- ☐ Avoidant of intimacy
- ☐ Conflictual
- ☐ Contemptuous
- ☐ Dysregulated

- ☐ Empathy Atypical/Deficient
- ☐ Entitled
- ☐ Egocentric
- ☐ Highly Conflictual
- ☐ Highly Reactive
- ☐ Hungry for Narcissistic Supply

- ☐ Inflammatory
- ☐ Manipulative
- ☐ Rigid
- ☐ Selfish
- ☐ Toxic
- ☐ Tyrannical

Catalog of Traits of Pathological Narcissists

- ☐ Abrasive
- ☐ Abrupt
- ☐ Abusive
- ☐ Addiction Susceptible
- ☐ Aggressive
- ☐ Amoral
- ☐ Angry
- ☐ Antagonistic
- ☐ Anxious
- ☐ Apathetic
- ☐ Argumentative
- ☐ Arrogant
- ☐ Asocial
- ☐ Authoritarian
- ☐ Belligerent

- ☐ Blaming of Others
- ☐ Blunt
- ☐ Boastful
- ☐ Boisterous
- ☐ Boorish
- ☐ Calculating
- ☐ Callous
- ☐ Careless
- ☐ Charming
- ☐ Charmless
- ☐ Coarse
- ☐ Cocky
- ☐ Cold
- ☐ Compulsive
- ☐ Conceited
- ☐ Condemnatory

- ☐ Condescending
- ☐ Conformist
- ☐ Conflictual
- ☐ Confrontational
- ☐ Contemptuous
- ☐ Controlling
- ☐ Crafty
- ☐ Crass
- ☐ Crude
- ☐ Cruel
- ☐ Cunning
- ☐ Cynical
- ☐ Deceitful
- ☐ Defensive
- ☐ Demanding
- ☐ Destructive

☐ Detached

☐ Devious

☐ Difficult

☐ Disagreeable

☐ Disconcerting

☐ Discontented

☐ Discouraging

☐ Discourteous

☐ Dishonest

☐ Disloyal

☐ Disputatious *(fond of causing arguments)*

☐ Disrespectful

☐ Disruptive

☐ Dissolute *(lax in morals)*

☐ Dissonant

☐ Distant

☐ Dogmatic

☐ Domineering

☐ Dysregulated

☐ Egocentric

☐ Empathy Atypical/ Deficient

☐ Entitled

☐ Envious

☐ Erratic

☐ Evasive

☐ Extravagant

☐ Extroverted

☐ Facetious

☐ Fanatical

☐ Fawning

☐ Fearful

☐ Flirtatious

☐ Forgetful

☐ Frightening

☐ Frivolous

☐ Gossipy

☐ Greedy

☐ Grumpy

☐ Harsh

☐ Hateful

☐ Haughty

☐ Hostile

☐ Humorless

☐ Hungry for Narcissistic Supply

☐ Hurtful

☐ Hypocritical

☐ Ignorant

☐ Illogical

☐ Impatient

☐ Impolite

☐ Impractical

☐ Impulsive

☐ Inattentive

☐ Inconsiderate

☐ Inconsistent

☐ Indifferent

☐ Indiscreet

☐ Inflammatory

☐ Inflexible

☐ Insecure

☐ Insensitive

☐ Insincere

☐ Insulting

☐ Interfering

☐ Intimacy Avoidant

☐ Intolerant

☐ Introverted

☐ Irrational

☐ Irresponsible

☐ Jealous

☐ Judgmental

☐ Know-It-All

☐ Lacking Integrity

☐ Licentious *(promiscuous, unprincipled in sexual matters)*

☐ Machiavellian

☐ Macho

☐ Malicious

☐ Manipulative

☐ Materialistic

☐ Mean

☐ Meddlesome

☐ Melodramatic

☐ Miserable

☐ Monstrous

☐ Moody

☐ Mysterious

☐ Narrow-minded

☐ Nasty

☐ Negative

☐ Neglectful

☐ Obnoxious

☐ Obsessive

☐ Obstinate

- [ ] Opinionated
- [ ] Over Charitable
- [ ] Overcritical
- [ ] Oversensitive
- [ ] Offensive
- [ ] Paranoid
- [ ] Passive-aggressive
- [ ] Patronizing
- [ ] Perfectionistic
- [ ] Perverse
- [ ] Pessimistic
- [ ] Petty
- [ ] Petulant
- [ ] Pompous
- [ ] Possessive
- [ ] Power-Hungry
- [ ] Predatory
- [ ] Prejudiced
- [ ] Pretentious
- [ ] Puritanical
- [ ] Pushy
- [ ] Quarrelsome
- [ ] Racist
- [ ] Reactive
- [ ] Reckless
- [ ] Repulsive
- [ ] Resentful
- [ ] Rigid
- [ ] Rude
- [ ] Ruthless
- [ ] Sanctimonious
- [ ] Scary
- [ ] Scornful

- [ ] Secretive
- [ ] Self-centered
- [ ] Self-destructive
- [ ] Self-indulgent
- [ ] Selfish
- [ ] Sexist
- [ ] Shallow
- [ ] Shameless
- [ ] Sleazy
- [ ] Sly
- [ ] Sneaky
- [ ] Snobbish
- [ ] Stingy
- [ ] Stubborn
- [ ] Superficial
- [ ] Suspicious
- [ ] Tactless
- [ ] Temperamental
- [ ] Tense
- [ ] Thoughtless
- [ ] Touchy
- [ ] Toxic
- [ ] Trivial
- [ ] Truculent (*quick to fight*)
- [ ] Tyrannical

- [ ] Unappreciative
- [ ] Uncaring
- [ ] Uncharitable
- [ ] Uncommunicative
- [ ] Uncooperative
- [ ] Uncouth
- [ ] Unethical
- [ ] Unfriendly
- [ ] Unforgiving
- [ ] Ungrateful
- [ ] Uninhibited
- [ ] Unkind
- [ ] Unpleasant
- [ ] Unrealistic
- [ ] Unreliable
- [ ] Unstable
- [ ] Untrustworthy
- [ ] Uptight
- [ ] Vague
- [ ] Vain
- [ ] Vengeful
- [ ] Vindictive
- [ ] Violent
- [ ] Volatile
- [ ] Vulgar
- [ ] Withdrawn

> **Growth Moment**
>
> If you have the companion guide to this book, the *Swimming with Sharks Growth Book*, take a moment here to check out the **Common Traits of Abusive Narcissists** activity.

Common Manipulation Tactics of a Pathological Narcissist

Below are common tactics used by pathological narcissists to get what they want. Not every narcissist will use each of them, but you have likely experienced quite a few when on the receiving end of narcissistic abuse (NAb).

Note: While the following behaviors are presented from the perspective of a narcissist exhibiting them, they are not limited only to narcissists. You may witness some of these behaviors from people who are not narcissists. It is also not uncommon for those in a relationship with or raised by a narcissist to develop some of these behaviors over time and still not be a pathological narcissist.

*Terms with an asterisk are ones that I created throughout the course of my work to help identify and describe patterns I was seeing in survivor-victims.

Coercively Controlling
Controlling and manipulative behavior that often intimidates or humiliates a person into giving up their freedom of choice and creates an unequal power dynamic. This is often seen as a pattern of behaviors that adds up over time. The result leaves the victim with a low sense of self-worth and very little confidence in their own independent decision-making abilities. Examples include gaslighting, controlling finances, constantly criticizing or belittling, isolation, monitoring activity, jealous accusations, parental alienation, blackmailing, and making violent threats, among others.

With coercive control, it is as though the narcissist locks you in their own little jail cell. They use threats and manipulation to maintain power and get their way or what they want. If it ever feels like the cell door is open, and you start to try to leave, they shove you back in, slam the door shut, and lock it.

31

Charming Others

The definition of this one is pretty self-explanatory, but you might be a little confused as to why this is listed under narcissists' tactics. Not every narcissist is charming, but those who are, use it as an extremely effective technique to draw people in as well as manipulate others in the subtlest of ways.

Deflecting and Distracting

Deflection is a distraction technique. It occurs when the narcissist is on the receiving end of an accusation or other statement that makes the narcissist uncomfortable, and they instead redirect the accusation toward someone or something else in order to avoid taking responsibility for whatever they did.

Deploying Flying Monkeys

This is when narcissists use other people to do their bidding, such as enlisting family members to convince you of something.

Devaluing

Treating you or what you care about as unimportant or unworthy. In addition to directly devaluing you, narcissists will often devalue the things and people that you like, as a means to either devalue you or increase their control over you.

Discarding

This occurs when a narcissist chooses to get rid of or cast you away as though you are useless. Narcissists often treat people in their lives like cars. They see people similarly to how one sees a shiny new car, exciting in the beginning, but as it ages, they want to trade it in for a new and better model. Cars are things though. It's okay to think of cars this way. You are a human being, and it's never okay to be treated this way.

Dismissing
Narcissists will often show indifference toward you or disregard the things you say, communicating to you that they don't see you or your ideas as worth their attention or consideration.

Distracting
Similar to what a magician might do to get you to temporarily focus your attention away from the trick, a narcissist uses this similarly as another manipulation tactic to avoid bringing attention to something they don't want to take ownership of or don't want you to see, or don't want to see in theirself.

Future Faking
This is another form of manipulation in which a narcissist promises something concerning your future, intending to get you to do what they want, but without the intention of following through on the promise.

Gaslighting
Planting seeds of doubt or manipulating information to make you question your memories, sanity, and/or perception of reality.

Unfortunately, this word seems to have become a catch-all for many different toxic behaviors and is often used incorrectly. Keep in mind that if the behavior you are trying to describe does not lead to the victim questioning their sense of reality, then it is not a form of gaslighting.

Hoovering
Used to suck you back into the relationship by any means necessary if they sense you pulling away.

Invalidating
This occurs when the narcissist denies, rejects, or dismisses your thoughts, feelings, beliefs, experience, etc. This can lead to you feeling confused and full of self-doubt.

Lying
Any form of lying is commonly used by narcissists as a manipulation tactic.

Love Bombing
Narcissists will attempt to influence you by showering you with over-the-top gifts, praise, accolades, attention, or affection.

Manipulating (Dysfunctional Manipulation*)
Intentionally implementing specific tactics to get what they want for dysfunctional and unhealthy reasons. Dysfunctional manipulation deviates from the social norms of functional manipulation. Each of the tactics in this list is a form of dysfunctional manipulation.

Mind Reading
Inferring or assuming what is going on in someone's mind without bothering to ask them what they are thinking or feeling.

Minimizing and Maximizing
Invalidating someone else's experience by making it seem unimportant or not taking responsibility for their actions or choices.

Or

Minimize what they do and maximize what you do and vice versa, depending on the context.

Mirroring
A narcissist will profess to have the same likes, dislikes, dreams, passions, hobbies, and more, to draw you in and promote a stronger bond, making it less likely for you to want to leave them.

Narcissist's Amnesia*
When a narcissist claims to not remember their abusive behaviors.

Narcissist's Delusion*
Narcissist's Delusion, on the other hand, occurs when a narcissist tells a lie so thoroughly and/or over such a long period, to theirself and/or to others, that they begin to believe that it's true. The narcissist's lie becomes their reality. They believe it so vehemently that they will swear by it up and down.

This is not to be confused with self-delusion, which occurs when someone tells theirself a falsehood to maintain their self-esteem. Self-delusion stems from insecurity and is often a means to maintain a grandiose view of oneself or ensure others have the same perspective.

Narcissist's Injury
This is what a narcissist experiences when they perceive themselves as being under attack or held accountable for their actions in such a way that threatens their self-image.

Narcissist's Rage
An intense overtly aggressive or passive-aggressive reaction to a narcissist's injury that has occurred. This often seems irrational and disproportionate to what occurred.

Narcissistic Supply Hopping*
Narcissistic supply is the emotional energy that other people provide to a narcissist. Narcissistic supply hopping occurs when a narcissist drains one person of their emotional energy reserves, feels like they can't get anything more from that person, and then moves on to another person to tap into their supply, and so forth. (Discussed in further detail in the chapter on Narcissistic Supply)

Projecting
A defense mechanism in which a narcissist will attribute or assign their traits or behaviors to someone else. This could also be considered another distraction technique.

Scapegoating
Unfairly placing blame on someone else for something they have not caused.

Shaming
Attempting to make you feel less worthy as a means to control you.

Spreading Falsehoods
Many narcissistic abusers will lie and speak poorly about you to others in both of your lives, mutual or non-mutual friends, family, and acquaintances. This could be in an attempt to shift the loyalty of your allies over to them. Or it could simply be for them to feel better about theirself. They may tell your closest confidants you're having an affair when you're not or call you mentally unstable and unfit to care for your children, even to lawyers and judges. They are capable of crafting any number of falsehoods if they think it's in their best interest.

Stonewalling
Occurs when the narcissist refuses to interact or communicate with you as a means to re-establish their control.

Tale Twisting*
Rather than sticking with the facts and looking at something objectively, the narcissist will twist **someone else's** words into the story that they want to tell. This is somewhat similar to gaslighting; however, it doesn't lead to anyone doubting their sanity or perception of reality, and it often involves people on the outside. For example, a narcissist might "tale twist" when explaining to a judge why they want custody of the children.

Triangulating
This occurs when there is conflict between the narcissist and someone else, and as a means to manipulate, they pull a third party into the conflict.

Victimizing
A form of distraction and manipulation to shift your focus away from their wrongdoings.

Now that you have a greater awareness of these traits and tactics, you will be able to more easily identify whether they are or are not occurring. If someone in your life demonstrates a consistent pattern of engaging in a number of the traits and tactics listed above, there is a good chance that they are a pathological narcissist. Be careful not to come to that conclusion too quickly or easily though. Educate yourself, seek professional counseling from someone qualified in NAb, and observe. Remember, displaying one or two of the traits or tactics once in a while does not make someone a narcissist. The

Growth Moment

If you have the companion guide to this book, the *Swimming with Sharks Growth Book*, take a moment here to check out the *Common Tactics of an Abusive Narcissist* and *Falsehoods* activities.

key to identifying that someone is a narcissist is recognizing a regular pattern of repeated behaviors and characteristics that negatively impact other people in their life, usually those closest to them.

Chapter 6

NARCISSISTIC ABUSE STRESS

N arcissistic abuse can affect anyone negatively if they come across it even just once in a while. But facing narcissistic abuse on an ongoing basis disrupts your well-being on an entirely different level. Regardless of the type of relationship, managing life with a narcissist in it is similar to standing in the shore break at the beach. Sometimes it's as easy as standing in calm water with no surf at all. Other times, it's like getting pummeled by one crashing wave after another. You try to remain upright and avoid getting knocked off your feet or sucked into an undertow, but doing so is much more difficult and draining than standing in calm water. It's also unrealistic to expect yourself to get out of the water afterward without experiencing physical, emotional, and mental exhaustion. This is similar to what you experience after conflictual interactions with a narcissist—you feel like your mind, body, and soul reach a state of both being drained of positive energy and water-logged by negative energy—similar to pruney fingers after spending too much time in the water.

When you experience a pattern of symptoms but aren't sure exactly what they stem from or even that they are related to one another at all, the next best thing to knowing how to fix the symptoms is finding out that there's a name for it. Over my years of working with survivor-victims of NAb, it has become increasingly clear that there needs to be greater awareness of the detrimental effects of narcissistic abuse. An important factor in educating the public and advocating for increased awareness is having common terms and language that everyone can use and understand. While some terms can be found online, none are used consistently, and I have not found any of them to be specific enough to be relevant, applicable, or appropriate for both clinical and nonclinical contexts. That is why I coined the term, Narcissistic Abuse Stress (NAb Stress, or NAbS). Later in the chapter, I'll share more details about how and why I chose this term specifically.

NAb Stress encompasses the breadth of cognitive, emotional,

behavioral, and survival reactions that are experienced as a result of ongoing narcissistic abuse. Below is a list of those I have identified thus far. I imagine and hope that these will be refined and added to over time as the mental health community adopts this new term and adapts it to improve its clinical use.

The Cognitive & Emotional Reactions of Narcissistic Abuse Stress

*Terms with an asterisk are ones that I created throughout the course of my work to help identify and describe patterns I was seeing in survivor-victims.

Trapped
It's not uncommon to feel trapped in many different ways when you are in a relationship with a narcissist. The obvious is feeling trapped in the relationship, but you may also feel trapped within yourself, within your home, within your life, etc. In addition, the narcissist often purposefully traps you so that you can be available to them when they decide they need you.

Unsure & Unsafe
Having a narcissist in your life is like living over a tectonic plate. You never know when the next shift will occur that leads to an earthquake. You have no way of predicting the timing or severity of the next outburst. This ultimately leads to not feeling emotionally safe.

Misunderstood
You may communicate in the healthiest and most direct way possible, yet a narcissist will inevitably still twist what you say around, whether intentionally or not. Sometimes, it feels like they aren't even hearing what you are saying. Do you know the blue light glasses that you can wear to filter out the blue light from a computer or phone

screen? It's almost as though the narcissist is wearing blue light glasses, and you are speaking in blue light, so they can't process anything you are saying. They only process what they want to hear.

Used

Because part of narcissistic abuse is taking advantage of others, survivor-victims are often left with a feeling of being used. As long as you have something to offer that they want, they stick around. You are supplying them with their narcissistic fix, similar to a drug addict getting their fix. This relates to narcissistic supply, which is explained further in Chapter 25.

Confusion

With one of the most common tactics of narcissists being gaslighting, you are likely to find yourself commonly in a state of confusion. This will be further exacerbated when you're called mentally unstable or crazy. After being told this over and over, you may begin to believe you are going crazy.

The good news is that these emotions, while uncomfortable, are often a healthy response to the abuse you experience. Their presence doesn't mean you're "going crazy." Instead, what you're feeling only proves that your human response system is working. Just like a car sends out a warning when its engine overheats, these emotions are your warning sign that something isn't right!

The longer you ignore those warnings, the worse things will become. The problem is, your narcissistic abuser will further belittle you because of the understandable emotions you experience. It's just a matter of time before those emotions bubble to the surface. And when that happens, the narcissist will invalidate how you're feeling. Until you're able to see through these tactics, you'll struggle all the more, not fully understanding why you feel the way you do.

Fear, Stress, Anxiety, Panic
The fear of "setting off" the narcissist leads to constant anxiety and stress, as well as frequent panic. You feel like you're walking on eggshells because you don't want to "make things worse."
Many, if not most, of the survivor-victims I've worked with also live with fear that they will be judged for having been in or for staying in an abusive relationship.

Hurt, Depression, Grief
The level of pain someone experiences while in a relationship with a narcissist cannot be overstated. And everyone deals with extreme hurt differently. You may lash out in anger when you normally wouldn't respond that way. You also may engage in time-wasting or mind-numbing activities.

Shame
The feeling of not being good enough or unworthy, shame, is one of the predominant emotions that victims of narcissistic abuse experience. Shame is often the result of repeatedly being told by that narcissist that you aren't good enough, that everything is your fault, and that you aren't worthy, among many other damaging messages.

In addition to damaging our self-worth, shame tricks us into thinking that we need to hide the abuse we are experiencing, which can subconsciously lead to the desire to isolate ourselves from others to avoid our shame being revealed. It's so important, though, that you remember that you are worthy no matter what, and you are strong within your vulnerability.

Anger
Anger is a survival mechanism. It is commonly the outward expression of fear, hurt, or shame. Expressing fear, hurt, or shame makes us vulnerable, and being vulnerable is uncomfortable. These emotions

can also be debilitating. Our brains are wired to draw on the emotion of anger to help us function through threatening situations, a.k.a., survive. We perceive vulnerability and debilitation as threatening, which means that fear, hurt, or shame can seem threatening to us. When the brain taps into anger, it causes adrenaline to course throughout our bodies, thus preparing us to fight, or in most cases, function. If you find yourself getting angry but not being sure why, try asking yourself if it may be that your anger is masking fear, hurt, or shame.

> ### 🖤 Growth Moment
>
> If you have the companion guide to this book, the *Swimming with Sharks Growth Book*, take a moment here to check out the *Feeling Words List* to help yourself identify the emotions you've been experiencing.

The Behavioral Reactions of Narcissistic Abuse Stress

*Terms with an asterisk are ones that I created throughout the course of my work to help identify and describe patterns I was seeing in survivor-victims.

Taking It Out on Someone Else

We often do this when we become so overwhelmed by our own emotions that we no longer have the bandwidth to keep our emotions inside and stay calm. This could manifest as yelling at the children just after getting into a fight with the narcissist. Or, if you have a narcissistic boss, you may end up acting frustrated at your coworkers or subordinates. There are any number of ways in which this manifests, and it can be on a spectrum from minimal to extreme.

Oftentimes though, our awareness of whether or not we take our emotions out on others is minimal. Consider asking someone you can trust to give you feedback on your behavior. They can act as a mirror, reflecting back to you how and when you may be doing this so that you can learn and grow from it. If you find yourself frequently taking your emotions out on others, you can reduce this by becoming more in tune with your inner experience and addressing those emotions directly. Journaling about them or talking to a therapist are only a couple of effective ways to help.

Isolating Oneself

When we are depressed, we avoid, and we isolate. When we feel shame, we want to hide and isolate. When we feel anxious, trapped, or unsafe, we hunker down and isolate. Isolation is such a common reaction to all of the emotions that are experienced as a result of NAb Stress.

Because this is an example of one of the unhealthy reactions, the best course of action you can take is to do the opposite. Reach out to anyone you know who can help bring you out of your shell of isolation. Once you crack that barrier you've created, it will start to crumble and make it easier and easier for you to break free.

You may isolate yourself from others out of fear of them hurting you as your narcissist does. This isolation can cause or deepen depression. In addition, the narcissist may attempt to isolate you from others to better control you. Worst of all, your hurts may become so severe that your thoughts become self-defeating and in the worst case can become suicidal.

You may find that you have been isolating yourself from others or that your narcissist has isolated you. It's common to wake up one day and wonder where everyone else in your life has gone. Isolating yourself could be the result of feeling like you need to hide the truth, the first pattern of NAb discussed.

Your narcissist may isolate you to control or dominate you so that you can continue to be their narcissistic supply. In many cases, the narcissist will practice several tactics to isolate you. If they are the type of narcissist who is controlling in this way, their attempts to cut you off from others may grow stronger if they feel you're beginning to wake up to what's happening. They are likely to fear losing control over you and may try to further limit whom you spend time with or obsessively monitor your social media, phone, and text interactions.

Hiding the Truth from Others

Hiding the truth often stems from fear of others judging us or of them judging the narcissist. Survivor-victims also hide the truth of what is really going on for fear that someone may pressure them to do something they don't want to do, like leave. Because narcissists are so skilled at exuding an image of success, wealth, or the perfect life, you may be concerned that those closest to you won't believe things are as bad as you claim. You may find yourself worried that others in your life will think you're overreacting and that things are far better than they are.

Shutting Down

It's normal for us to shut down as a defense mechanism. Without realizing it, we do this when we feel unsafe. Sometimes, it's protective. Sometimes, it's used as a means to pause and assess in order to best determine our next course of action. While shutting down isn't inherently unhealthy or dysfunctional, if you notice it lasting for long periods of time or leading to isolation or avoidance of positive things in your life, it has transitioned from healthy to unhealthy.

Avoidance

Avoidance of the narcissist or situations that we fear may lead to flare-ups of narcissistic abuse is a common choice to protect oneself from further abuse.

Overuse of Substances
Food and other substance overuse are common maladaptive coping mechanisms for any number of issues we face but especially when we are trying to make ourselves feel better because we feel stuck in a narcissistically abusive relationship.

Secondary Narcissist*
This reaction occurs when the non-narcissist has spent so much time with a narcissist that, without realizing it, they take on the same behaviors as the narcissist. This is most common in adult children and long-term partners of narcissists.

Narcissist-by-Proxy*
This reaction is seen when the non-narcissist has spent so much time with a narcissist that their level of codependence leads the non-narcissist to implement the narcissist's behaviors in lieu of the narcissist. Sometimes this is part of serving the narcissist's bidding, similar to Flying Monkey, but it can also occur without the prompting of the narcissist. Oftentimes, the non-narcissist will function as a Narcissist-by-Proxy out of anticipation of the narcissist's reaction to a given circumstance.

The Survival Reactions of Narcissistic Abuse Stress

*Terms with an asterisk are ones that I created throughout the course of my work to help identify and describe patterns I was seeing in survivor-victims.

Suppression of Emotions
Suppression of feelings is a survival mechanism that is often misused. I say that it is misused because it is only meant to be put to

use for very short periods when you are under attack or otherwise threatened. However, when pent-up emotions are suppressed long enough because we don't feel safe sharing our authentic feelings, we often become so frustrated that we are no longer able to contain the emotions. At this point, they may come out as anger or manifest within our bodies as ailments or maladies.

Narcissistic Abuse Amnesia*

We are wired to survive by avoiding danger and things that are unhealthy for us. Enduring the behaviors exhibited by a narcissist and choosing to stay in a relationship with them is difficult for our brains to reconcile. Our minds often react by forgetting how we are treated over and over so that we don't have to feel at odds with our decision to endure continued abuse. It is a sort of amnesia to what happens within a narcissistic relationship.

To give a rather extreme analogy, it is similar to being set on fire by the narcissist. Afterward, they extinguish the fire, and you're so thankful for them "saving you" that you completely disregard the fact that they were the one who set you on fire in the first place.

Survival Manipulation*

The term manipulation is typically used with a negative connotation and is considered to be dysfunctional. However, manipulation is actually a regular part of each of our everyday lives. We just don't think of what we are doing as manipulative. To explore this, let me first share how I define manipulation.

If we consider manipulation as choosing or changing one thing in order to influence the outcome of another thing, then we can easily see how our choices throughout each day are a form of manipulation, which I refer to as "Functional Manipulation." We praise our kids in order to get them to continue cleaning their rooms. We speak kindly to our boss with the hope that they will treat us kindly in return. We learn to phrase requests or feedback in ways that are most likely to elicit a positive response. Have you heard of the "sandwich method," where you share something negative in between two positives? These examples are all forms of manipulation which, as you can see, can be functional and are not necessarily bad. Sometimes we are aware that we are doing these things and other times we are not.

Survival manipulation, on the other hand, occurs when someone makes certain choices or behaves in certain ways with the hope that the narcissist will not become enraged or otherwise behave poorly. The purpose of this manipulation is to exist within a narcissistic relationship with as little conflict as possible, i.e. survive! Typically, someone will have some level of awareness that this is what they are doing, they just wouldn't have known to call it this. Survival manipulation is formulated cognitively, as opposed to the next type of manipulation which is more emotionally based.

Hypervigilant Manipulation*
Hypervigilant Manipulation is an anxious type of functional manipulation used to avoid conflict with the narcissist. Examples of this include rushing around the house to quickly pick up all the toys just before you know the narcissist is supposed to arrive home. Sometimes you may also notice yourself hushing the children as their volume increases, in an attempt to avoid the narcissist yelling at them.

With hypervigilant manipulation, you are trying to anticipate both the needs and the outbursts of the narcissist, in order to avoid experiencing any of their abusive behavior, whether it's yourself who would be on the receiving end or others.

Extreme Validation*
Another form of functional manipulation, Extreme Validation is when you go overboard in validating the narcissist. This can be

used in conjunction with setting boundaries in an effort to encourage behavioral changes in the narcissist.

For example, you might set a boundary by telling the narcissist that you will no longer tolerate them raising their voice at you during an argument. The next time you have an argument, you notice that they didn't raise their voice this time, so you shower them with praise and appreciation afterward for keeping their voice calm. Then you follow up with additional praise and validation the following day by once again expressing appreciation for them maintaining a calm voice during your disagreement.

By implementing this type of extreme validation, you are not only positively reinforcing the behavioral change you want to see, you are also validating the narcissist theirself, building up their self-image which is the underlying cause of the narcissistic behavior to begin with.

> **Growth Moment**
>
> If you have the companion guide to this book, the *Swimming with Sharks Growth Book*, take a moment here to check out the **Narcissistic Abuse Stress** Checklist & Reflection page.

To Name a Disorder or Not?

Growing up the child of a narcissist or being an adult in any sort of relationship with a narcissist can sometimes feel like you're facing psychological warfare. It's just that others don't see the explosions and ensuing destruction. While prolonged exposure to narcissistic abuse is traumatic, posttraumatic stress disorder (PTSD) is rarely the appropriate diagnosis, unless the victim was also exposed to an event that involved actual or threatened death, serious injury, or sexual violence. Even if this were so, a diagnosis of PTSD would relate to the symptoms that resulted from that event; however, it still wouldn't accurately address the specific disturbances and alterations in functioning that are unique to ongoing narcissistic abuse.

Concerns have been raised among a few of my colleagues over the idea of creating a diagnosable "disorder" with which survivor-victims can be labeled because there is a risk that it could then be used as ammunition against them. The concerns specifically stem from fear that pathological narcissists will try to use the label of a disorder against the survivor-victims during court cases such as divorce, custody, and domestic violence cases in which the narcissist is the perpetrator of the abuse. While this concerns me as well, I believe more strongly in the potential benefits that can come from the awareness that a diagnosis provides. If there is a diagnosable disorder that the medical and psychological communities recognize, then more providers will become aware of it, increasing the number of people who are afflicted with the symptoms of Narcissistic Abuse Stress to be identified and helped. Furthermore, this also improves the likelihood that mental health providers will progressively receive education and training in the knowledge and treatment of NAb Stress, something that I am looking forward to further developing and providing.

Anticipating that a diagnosis will do much more good than harm, I wanted to create a name that made practical and clinical sense based on linguistics research and the precedents already set by characterizations of similar collections of symptoms. My first question was whether or not to use the term "disorder" or "syndrome," as I have seen quoted in articles online. "Syndrome" doesn't feel adequate because it simply refers to a collection of symptoms. It doesn't specifically speak to the distress and impact on daily functioning that ongoing narcissistic abuse causes. The World Health Organization characterizes a mental disorder as a "clinically significant disturbance in an individual's cognition, emotional regulation, or behavior. It is usually associated with distress or impairment in important areas of functioning."[2]

---

[2]"Mental Disorders." World Health Organization, World Health Organization, 8 June 2022, https://www.who.int/news-room/fact-sheets/detail/mental-disorders#-:~:text=A%20mental%20disorder%20is%20characterized,different%20types%20of%20mental%20disorders.

"Disorder" clearly made more sense, as it is an apt description of the impact that narcissistic abuse has on countless individuals. At this point, I still hadn't developed the term "Narcissistic Abuse Stress" and would just refer to "narcissistic abuse," so I decided to review the anxiety and stress disorders again. It was at this point that I realized that modeling the name and criteria after acute stress disorder and posttraumatic stress disorder made the most sense. It was with this in mind that I coined the term previously introduced, "Narcissistic Abuse Stress (NAb Stress, or NAbS)," as well as the potentially controversial but likely mental health field-changing, "Narcissistic Abuse Stress Disorder (NAbSD)."

Identifying Narcissistic Abuse Stress Disorder

While this has not yet been submitted to the American Psychiatric Association's Committee on Psychiatric Diagnosis and Assessment for consideration to be included in the DSM-V, I have created a set of proposed diagnostic criteria to be used to identify the presence of Narcissistic Abuse Stress Disorder (NAbSD).

I want to reiterate that the criteria for diagnosis of this disorder were developed from two main factors. Firstly, they are based on my clinical experience providing psychotherapy to survivor-victims of narcissistic abuse since 2013, during which I have observed, documented, and tracked the effects of narcissistic abuse on each of these patients. Over time, clear and distinctive patterns emerged within the clinical anecdotal evidence, illustrating commonalities in the experiences of those who are targets of narcissistic abuse. Secondly, I integrated these identified patterns into a familiar framework, using the stress disorders that are currently present in the DSM-V as a model (i.e. PTSD & Acute Stress Disorder). The criteria have **not** been developed from any formal academic or clinical studies.

The following includes a list of symptoms that are commonly

present in Narcissistic Abuse Stress Disorder (NAbSD). Not every-one will experience each of the symptoms listed, and symptoms may change over time. Similar to official diagnoses found in the DSM-V, to qualify for a diagnosis of Narcissistic Abuse Stress Disorder, the symptoms would need to be present at a level that causes significant distress or impairment of personal and/or inter-personal areas of functioning.

Psychological Symptoms

⚓ Presence of any of the following symptoms related to mental functioning:

⚓ Difficulty concentrating, frequently distracted.

⚓ Intrusive memories or flashbacks of occurrences of nar-cissistic abuse.

⚓ Presence of any of the following numbing symptoms:

⚓ Difficulty experiencing positive emotions.

⚓ Decreased interest in activities that once interested you outside of the narcissistic relationship.

⚓ Feeling isolated from others outside of your relationship.

⚓ Mental and emotional crash after interacting with the narcissist.

⚓ Neglecting one's own hobbies and interests in order to mold oneself to the desires of the narcissist. Sometimes to the point of forgetting your own interests.

⚓ Narcissistic Abuse Amnesia—a purposeful and some-times subconscious forgetting of repeated abuse, or will-fully ignoring the fault of the abuser in their choice to engage in abusive behavior.

⚓ Presence of any of the following fear-based symptoms:

   ⚓ Persistent levels of heightened anxiety, particularly when anticipating the narcissist returning home or anticipating them responding poorly to something.

   ⚓ Emotional distress after reminders of the abuse or the abuser.

   ⚓ Avoidance of narcissistic abuse-related thoughts, feelings, or external reminders.

   ⚓ Avoidance of allowing oneself to think of the narcissist as an abuser.

   ⚓ Avoidance of openly sharing with others what you are experiencing.

   ⚓ Excessive worrying that no one will understand if you do share.

   ⚓ Avoidance of new relationships out of fear that they will be a narcissist too.

⚓ Presence of any of the following symptoms resulting from negative experiences with others:

   ⚓ Lingering discomfort after telling one or more people outside of the relationship private details about the narcissistic abuse and then experiencing them doubting the truth of what you say. May lead to worry and avoidance of being vulnerable in the future or with other people.

⚓ Presence of any of the following symptoms related to self-esteem:

   ⚓ Overly negative thoughts or assumptions about oneself or the world, pessimistic (i.e. anticipating everyone else will be a narcissist).

   ⚓ Blaming oneself for the narcissistic abuse.

⚓ Diminished self-esteem, sometimes to the point of seemingly nonexistent.

⚓ Questioning of one's own sanity, particularly after confrontations with the narcissist.

Behavioral Symptoms

⛵ Avoidance of conflict with the narcissist.

⚓ Holding in thoughts and feelings for so long that, eventually, they erupt all at once, causing one to "blow up" at the narcissist, and subsequently experiencing shame, regret, and self-blame, which can last for years, even if the relationship has ended.

⚓ Hypervigilant in avoiding anything that might set off the narcissist. This includes one's own behaviors, choices, actions, communication, and social media posts, as well as others' behaviors, choices, actions, and communication.

⚓ Making sure that things are "just right," whether that's around the house, with the kids or siblings, one's own academic or work performance, etc., in order to avoid conflict with the narcissist.

⛵ Presenting a false image of yourself and/or your family to the rest of the world.

⚓ Feeling the need to present an image of your family or relationship that is consistent with the false image that the narcissist presents to others.

⚓ Filtering social media posts of anything that might indicate to others that there is something wrong.

⚓ Avoid sharing honest information with others, even those closest to you, about your relationship difficulties.

⚓ Increasingly isolating oneself from others outside of the narcissistic relationship.

⚓ Suppression of emotions to the extent that it leads to an eventual outburst of feelings or to a suspected manifestation of maladies or ailments within the body.

⚓ Aggressive and/or disproportionate responses, such as impulsively snapping, typically toward family members other than the narcissist, such as children, siblings, the other parent, coworkers, or friends.

⚓ Impulsively becoming physically aggressive in reaction to narcissistically abusive behaviors, such as shoving.

⚓ Adoption of Survival Tactics such as Survival Manipulation, including Hypervigilant Manipulation and Extreme Validation.

🐟 **Growth Moment**

Check to see if you have NabSD—Open the *Identifying Narcissistic Abuse Stress Disorder* checklist in the companion guide to this book, *Swimming with Sharks Growth Book.*

Chapter 7

NARCISSISTIC
ABUSE IS STILL ABUSE

T his is one of the saddest perspectives I come across in my work. It breaks my heart to hear that someone believes that it would be more valid to leave an abuser if that abuse were physical. Somehow, society has led so many of us to believe that physical abuse counts and psychological abuse doesn't. That simply is not true.

Even If You're Not Being Hit, It's Still Abuse!

It's important that you understand that abuse can exist even when there is no physical violence. I definitely don't want to downplay physical abuse. Physical abuse is dangerous. It takes one wrong shove, one hit to the head in just the wrong place, for you to be swiftly lifted out of this world. If you are experiencing physical violence, there are many resources available that you need to use. This book is not one of those. I do not have the training nor experience to even begin to adequately address how to handle that.

"I wish they would just hit me.
That way I could leave."

—Multiple anonymous patients

However, if you are experiencing physical abuse, call the number below for guidance.

*National Domestic Violence Hotline 24/7 at 800-799-7233

Narcissistic Traits + Tactics = Narcissistic Abuse

My expertise lies in the area of psychological abuse, specifically, narcissistic abuse. The ongoing, sneaky, underhanded abuse that creeps up on you without you even realizing it's there. The one that masquerades as a righteous course corrector. The one that masks itself as something with which you are comfortable because you re- member hearing similar scoldings from your parents. However, even if those scoldings might have been appropriate from a parent, these types of confrontations from a partner or other adult relation- ship are never appropriate.

Psychological abuse hurts every bit as much as physical abuse, just in a different way. Being called things like stupid, worthless, ugly, lazy, fat, pitiful, angry, pathetic, a failure, not good enough, and the like have a different impact than being hit. These wounds pierce deep into your soul and crush your spirit. They're an attack on the core of who you are. These words lead you to question your- self, doubt yourself, and begin to believe them as reality. They tear you down, rip you apart, and leave you lying on the floor, bleeding out, with no one to pick you up and repair the wounds but yourself.

You may not want to hear this, but PLEASE, hear *these words* if you take nothing else from this book . . .

You are in an abusive relationship.
Your partner [or other relationship] is abusive.
You are a victim of abuse.
But you can and you will survive that abuse.
You just have to be the one to rescue yourself.
No one else will.
No one else can.
Especially not the narcissist.
So STOP waiting!

For those of you who believe in God, you may have read my words above and instinctively reacted in disagreement, knowing that God can rescue you. You may be waiting for a miracle. Thinking that if you pray hard enough, long enough, your partner will one day change. Or you may think that God will send someone to save you one of these days. Here is what I know of God though. While God has the power to change anything, He gave you the ability to make your own choices. Yes, He will put circumstances and people in your life for you to use as tools to help lift you out of your situation, but ultimately, He also gave you free will, which means that you can choose to make change happen.

For all of you, regardless of religion or faith, it is up to *you* to *will* yourself out of the abuse. *Willing* yourself out of abuse takes several steps:

> **Step One:** Acknowledge the reality of the abuse.
> **Step Two:** *Want* change. *Choose* change. *Decide* to make a change.
> **Finally**, it requires *you* to take action.

 Growth Moment

Take a moment here to do some journaling about your perspective on having been abused and what your thoughts are regarding making a change.

Part Three

Surviving
Narcissist-Infested
Waters

Chapter 8

THE THREE STEPS TO WILL YOURSELF OUT OF NARCISSISTIC ABUSE

Step One: Acknowledge the Reality of the Abuse

Whether it is because they don't like the idea of admitting that the person they love is abusive, or they are uncomfortable seeing theirself as someone who has allowed theirself to be abused, many people I come across struggle greatly using the word abuse. Just remember, the fact that you are being abused is not a reflection on you at all. It does not mean that you are any less of a person. But as we talked about in the last chapter, being attacked over and over by someone who is using narcissistic tactics means that you are being abused. Once you are able to acknowledge this, it frees you to move on to the next phase, wanting, choosing, and deciding to make a change.

Step Two: Want, Choose, and Decide to Make a Change

Change isn't easy. In fact, the thing that I remember most from my first psychology class ever, during my sophomore year of high school, is that the number one fear people have is change. Not flying. Not heights. Not public speaking. Not dying. CHANGE!

However, change is arguably the very essence of life, of existence. Nothing stays the same, not even for a moment. Our bodies are forever changing. Every atom, making up every molecule, making up every substance in the world is in a state of constant and perpetual change, simply by the fact that electrons are always in motion. Our minds are changing every moment as one thought leads to another. Even laying in stillness, we are in motion, as our involuntary systems move to keep us alive. So if moving forward (change)—the very antithesis to remaining frozen in time—is part of our essential makeup and how we and everything around us were designed to function, then tell me, why are we so afraid of change?

One answer is that it doesn't matter why. What matters is that we stop being afraid of it. Another answer is that we are afraid of change because we don't know what to expect. This means we don't feel like we can be prepared to handle what comes after the change. This leads to anxiety, which is extremely uncomfortable. The solution to both of these answers?

ACCEPT the fear. ACCEPT the unknown. Rest in the knowledge that we are designed to handle anything that comes our way. That's why our brains work so quickly. We are made to process things instantly and react accordingly. And finally, ACCEPT the *idea* of CHANGE. Once we are able to accept change itself, we will no longer have anything to fear, and fear will no longer be able to hold us back!

"FEAR IS THE ABSENCE OF ACCEPTANCE."

Once you release your fear of change, you'll be able to transition into a state of *wanting* change. Wanting change isn't quite enough though, because even if you want it, you still have the choice between change and no change. So actively *choosing* change is the next step. Finally, for change to actually happen, you'll have to *decide* to make a change. With decision comes intention, and action follows. Deciding means you opt for one option and eliminate all others as possibilities. When you've decided on change, it becomes your only way forward. Change becomes your destination. You don't need to know yet *how* you'll be moving forward toward that destination. As long as you know where you plan to end up, how to get there will come to you on the journey. Just start moving in that direction—take *action.*

Step Three: Take Action

You decided to make a change! Yay! You're on the journey toward soul-mending!

Now, it's time to ***Take Action.***

While this is very exciting, it is also difficult and trying. Part of taking action is determining whether or not you want to continue swimming in the water with the shark or get out of the water to safety. Lots of sources available online will make it seem as though there is only one right option: get out. However, I know that there are many different layers of this dilemma for you. Swimming away from a narcissist, regardless of their relation to you (partner, parent, friend, boss, etc.), is one of the most difficult choices you could face. This choice could create life-altering changes for not just you but others as well. I understand this is not a decision you want to make lightly, and hearing other people tell you that you need to leave is not always convincing or helpful. In fact, it can often feel very invalidating.

While you are evaluating the options before you, the most effective action you can take in the meantime is to begin to set boundaries, or build a shark cage around you. Setting boundaries and enforcing them will take incredible amounts of strength though. You will often feel as though you are swimming against the current.

Boundaries, however, will be your means to regaining control of your life and how you are treated. They will be your saving grace during any phase of this journey.

 Growth Moment

If you have the companion guide to this book, the *Swimming with Sharks Growth Book,* take a moment here to check out the ***Willing Yourself Out of Narcissistic Abuse*** Reflection Page.

Chapter 9

EVALUATING YOUR OPTIONS

As I mentioned earlier, the third step to willing yourself out of narcissistic abuse, taking action, is complicated. You likely feel the pressure to decide whether to maintain a relationship with the narcissist or step away from the relationship. It's one of the most difficult decisions you'll ever have to make, and it's nearly impossible to know which is the right choice, so fully evaluating your options is essential. Don't expect yourself to choose quickly, and know that it's normal to waffle back and forth. Grace and patience for yourself are essential at this moment.

Option 1: Treading Water

Sometimes we choose to stay simply because we don't want to change our situation or because we genuinely want to stay with the narcissist, and it feels like the right choice. Sometimes we stay in the water because we're either too afraid to get out of the water or we're too afraid to leave the shark.

Not Wanting to Get Out of the Water

You know how kids are when it's time to get out of the pool during the summer? Even if they're tired and exhausted, sun-burned, or scraped up, they will do whatever they can to get you to let them stay in just a few more minutes. They have no idea what fun is left to be had in the pool, and they desperately don't want to take a chance of missing out on it. It's easy for those of us on the outside to see that it's healthiest for them to exit the water, but they don't have the insight to gain that awareness.

Even though you've been badly hurt and burned, and you're tired and exhausted, you may still love and care for the narcissist in your life. Of course you wouldn't want to leave someone you love. On the surface, it wouldn't make sense to let go of a loved one. On top of that, you still aren't sure if they will end up changing in the end. You can't help but hope that there is still fun, joy, and love to be had in your relationship. This leaves you caught between wanting to stay and wondering if leaving is best. And, for the moment at least, not wanting to leave holds more power over you. You've also likely invested months or years of your life into this relationship and don't want to be "a quitter." You'd rather stick it out and try your best for a happy ending. On top of that, if kids are involved, you feel pressure to keep the family together. You don't want to break up the family unit unless you absolutely have to. All of these concerns are weighty and understandable. Additionally, there are many other potential social, spiritual, or financial reasons you may want to stay.

Fear of Getting Out of the Water

There are many reasons you may fear breaking free from your

narcissistically abusive relationship. Fear of making a mistake, fear of missing out on the life you envisioned for yourself, fear of the narcissist finding someone else, fear of surviving on your own, fear of how divorce looks, fear of splitting up the family, fear of scandal that could impact the ability of the narcissist to continue to provide for you and your family, and fear of being judged by others are all commonly experienced.

Because of the ongoing abuse you've endured, you may have become so dependent on the narcissist, or your self-image may be so low that you truly feel like you can't figure out the logistics of leaving. Furthermore, the idea of starting over may feel insurmountable.

Many survivor-victims of narcissistic parents and partners don't want to leave because they are afraid to break up their families. This can stem from concern over the impact on their children's development, fear of disappointing family members or being rejected by them, or fear of being rejected by others within your community (religious organization, group of friends, social circles, etc.). Some people even fear spiritual consequences, ranging from disappointing God to going to Hell.

Fear of What the Shark Might Do

You may also fear how your narcissist will react to your decision to end the relationship. Depending on the type of narcissistic abuser you're dealing with, you may fear for your emotional or physical safety. You may be concerned that the narcissist will try to turn family members against you, blackmail you, speak lies about you, "steal" your children (by manipulatively gaining custody), falsely incriminate you, or even physically injure you or your children. Not one of these fears is irrational. Not only have I worked with so many people who have feared these reactions, I've seen these things actually happen. Narcissistic partners often try to turn the children against their partner, while a narcissistic parent may try to turn the other parent, siblings, and extended family against you. Is this scary? Yes. But knowing what you could face and un-

derstanding the nature of the shark allows you to be better prepared for what may happen.

Shame over Staying

Many people are afraid of being judged for wanting to remain in
a relationship with a narcissist, particularly a narcissistic partner.
While it's pretty unlikely that I would say this to you if you were in
the water with an actual shark, I do want to reassure you that it is
okay if you feel like you want to stay in your relationship. I've witnessed a lot of shame around this, but I know that until someone is
fully ready to get out of the water and leave the shark behind, I
would only be hurting them if I pushed them to leave any sooner.
While fearing that I will judge them no longer surprises me, and I
understand why, it still breaks my heart that any of my patients
would fear being open with me, their therapist.

As you begin to share your situation with friends and family,
some of them may be tempted to think that they know best and are
entitled to have a say in your choice. The
choice to permanently leave a relationship
with a narcissist may seem like it would
be an easy decision to those outside
of the relationship, but in
reality, it can take months and
even years to get to that
point, if ever. You don't
need to feel guilty about
wanting to stay. Your
family and friends may
have their opinions. They
may even pressure you
one way or the other. None
of them has the right to
control or judge you for your
choice though. Ultimately,
you're the only one who can make

that decision. And you're the one whose life could be defined by that decision, not anyone else's. You really can't leave until you're ready, and there's no shame in that!

Option 2: Reeling Yourself Out of the Water

> ### 🐟 Growth Moment
>
> If you have the companion guide to this book, the *Swimming with Sharks Growth Book*, take a moment here to check out the handout for friends and family, *"What I Need You to Do or Not Do"* and *"What You Need to Know."*

It may take you a while to come to this decision, or it might be quick and easy. Narcissistic abuse can make it feel like you're being held underwater and leaving is the only way to breathe again. No matter how you've been impacted, one thing is certain, you are escaping out of a need to protect yourself and/or to protect others. This is an extremely difficult choice, but it will ultimately lead you on a path toward a healthier life. It does not come without consequences though. Many of which will be discussed later in the book. I think it's important though that we go ahead and address the shame that many experience.

Shame Over Getting Out

I mentioned earlier that many partners of narcissists feel shame over their desire to stay in their relationship. The same is often true for those who want to swim away, particularly those who are dealing with a narcissistic parent. Adult children of narcissists are frequently shamed by others when they decide that it's no longer healthy for their parent to remain an active part of their life. I can't tell you how many times a patient has shared with me that one of their friends or family members said some version of,

> "But you have to honor your mother/father."

> "You can't abandon them. That would be a horrible thing for you to do."

> "They gave you life. It's your obligation to love them and be there for them."

It's tragic to me any time I hear of someone being shamed, and this scenario is no exception. In fact, it actually makes me really mad that a victim of a narcissistically abusive parent would have to experience this because it only adds to the layers of trauma they've already had to endure their entire life.

Remember, deciding to get out of the water and escape to safety is *your* decision and yours alone. Please don't let the shame other people place on you affect your decision or impact how you feel about yourself. You have survived this long because you are amazing no matter what.

> **⬥ Growth Moment**
>
> If you have the companion guide to this book, the *Swimming with Sharks Growth Book*, take a moment here to check out the *"What I Need You to Not Say"* handout for friends and family.

Option 3: One Foot In, One Foot Out

It's very normal to experience a period of time when you have no idea what to do because neither staying nor leaving feels like the right choice. When you have no idea what to do, ask yourself the following question:

"What Would I Do
If I Weren't Afraid?"

If you are struggling to figure out whether staying or leaving is best for you, "What would I do if I weren't afraid?" is a really great question to ask yourself. It helps clarify what your inner voice is telling you—what your mind and heart truly know is best for you.

Honestly, this is simply a great question to ask ourselves daily. Fear is meant to protect us from harm, not hold us back from making healthy changes in our lives or achieving our aspirations. In reality though, fear is a great deceiver. It pops up and makes us think that it's protecting us, so we buy into it.

I know fear is about the only thing that holds me back from reaching my potential. Over the past couple of years, I've become keenly aware of my desire to be able to speak to large groups of people. Unfortunately, I have a pattern of avoiding opportunities to do so. I used to tell myself that it was just because I didn't have a desire to speak in public. But when I ask myself, "What would I do if I weren't afraid?" the answer is a resounding: "Get up and talk to as many groups of people as I can, in order to share the valuable knowledge, insights, and conclusions I've made through my work as a psychotherapist." This is how I know when fear is holding me back.

Now that you have a much better understanding of what to expect in your narcissistic relationship, and as you are considering how you want to move forward in your life, try asking *yourself,* "What would I do if I weren't afraid?" The answer to this question will give you the strongest insight into where your heart truly feels led.

 Growth Moment

If you have the companion guide to this book, the *Swimming with Sharks Growth Book,* take a moment here to work through the Reflection Page, *Evaluating Your Options.*

Chapter 10

KEEPING YOUR HEAD ABOVE WATER: HANDLING CONFRONTATIONS WITH NARCISSISTS

Survival 101: Setting Boundaries

When patients come to see me, they are either still in their narcissistic relationship, or they have moved on and are trying to heal. Most who are still in the relationship are looking for help in how to make the relationship work. They want to stay with the person who gave them life, or they want to stay with the person with whom they had planned to spend the rest of their life. However, what they don't want is to continue to endure the attacks, the abuse. It's at this point that they all feel at a loss, not knowing what they can do to move forward without losing themselves. I share with each of them that setting boundaries is the best way I have found for anyone to survive keeping a narcissist in their life.

First rule of surviving a narcissist . . .

Timing can be precarious when it comes to setting boundaries and can depend on your situation, the type of relationship you are in, the type of narcissist with which you are dealing, and whether you are trying to stay in the relationship or exit. Please make sure you read the rest of Part Four on Surviving Infested Waters before you begin making drastic changes in your boundaries, so you can make informed decisions on which boundaries to set and how best to set them.

Boundaries and Domestic Violence

Before we continue discussing boundaries, I want to explain that if you are experiencing domestic violence, you need to disregard this section. If that is the case, reach out to a local therapist and organization that supports and educates the public on how to safely handle domestic violence. Boundaries can escalate conflict and have the potential to inflame the narcissist. If they already commit physical acts of violence against you, attempting to set boundaries can become dangerous.

If you can, go to a shelter where you (and your children and pets if you have them) will be safe. Talk to law enforcement about how to protect yourself. I can't tell you how many women have told me that they regretted not calling the police in the past because once it came time to fight for custody of their children in court, they had no legal evidence of the violence. And unfortunately, the legal system is not known to work in the victim's favor or to understand how to protect children in these types of custody battles.

Again, if you or someone you know is experiencing domestic violence, please call the hotline number below.

*National Domestic Violence Hotline 24/7 at 800-799-7233

ALENA SCIGLIANO

Staring Down the Shark

Valerie Taylor, an inspiring Australian woman and marine conservationist, has spent much of her life literally swimming with sharks. She tells a fascinating story of how she, along with her husband and two other cameramen, aggressively established their presence while in a harrowing situation in which they were surrounded by hundreds of sharks. She described "fighting back" by hitting them with a club, punching them in the gills, bumping the sharks harder whenever they themselves were bumped, and holding firm. As Valerie explains it, knowledge that the humans would fight seemingly spread throughout the group of sharks. Within a matter of minutes, they were able to swim right alongside the sharks, even while the animals were feeding on a whale. Valerie also describes being able to train sharks by feeding them fish when they would behave as she wanted and knocking them on the head when they didn't.[3]

In each of these scenarios, Valerie understood and accepted the nature of the sharks. She survived by setting and enforcing boundaries that communicated to the sharks which behavior was acceptable and which wasn't. Similarly, Valerie advises swimmers

[3] Taylor, Valorie. "10 Myths about Sharks Debunked." *Australian Geographic*, 6 Feb. 2018, https://www.australiangeographic.com.au/topics/wildlife/2018/02/10-myths-about-sharks-the-truth/.

who confront a shark but don't have a means of escape to look the shark in the eye and act as aggressively as possible. She aptly points out that most attacks occur before the shark is seen, but if you see the shark first, your most difficult hurdle is your own fear.

Facing the Shark and "Holding Firm"

Setting boundaries and standing up to your narcissist is scary, just as facing a shark and assertively looking them in the eye would be frightening. It's risky. You don't know what to expect. I can't speak for what would happen the first time you assert your presence with a shark versus the second or third time. But I can tell you that it is common to receive a strongly negative reaction to your assertiveness the first time you put it into practice with a narcissist. However, it is typical for this to subside as you continue to assert the same boundary over and over. The narcissist will begin to adapt, much like the sharks adapted to Valerie's boundaries.

I'd like to remind you at this point that, just as a shark won't turn into a dolphin when you start getting aggressive with it, a narcissist won't turn into Prince, Princess, or PrinceX Charming. Even though there may be periods of time when they seem to improve, the narcissist will always be a narcissist. The point of setting boundaries is simply to limit the narcissistically abusive behavior to which you are subjected—and to survive.

Enforcing Boundaries

I can say with 100 percent certainty that, at one time or another, your narcissist will attempt to violate most if not all of the boundaries you set. Initially, it may be difficult to hold the narcissist accountable for broken boundaries. You may be tempted to ignore the offense, reverting back to your former role of ignoring the abuse for the sake of peace. You also may be tempted to lash out or express your hurt or frustration in a passive-aggressive manner. Neither of these options is effective though. The best way to address a disregarded boundary is to enforce it by calmly interjecting in order to pause or interrupt the flow of the interaction, and gently remind the narcissist of the boundary. If necessary, the reminder may need to be stated more firmly.

Electrifying the Fence

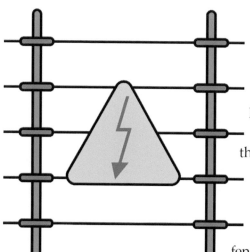

Fences can be small and serve the purpose of marking the boundaries of your property, or they can be large and fixed to fully keep intruders out. Regardless of the size though, if someone wants to get on your property, they're not going to care that your fence is there.

Boundaries are like fences. Narcissists will try to cross any boundary you set and think nothing of it. They only respect a boundary if, like a fence, you electrify it, i.e. establish a consequence. Whenever they try to cross it, they get an electric shock i.e. follow through on enforcing the consequence. As you establish your boundaries, inform the narcissist that there will be a consequence if a boundary is broken, and state what the consequence will be. For example, "If you don't stop yelling at me, I'm going to walk away." Keep in mind though, respecting your boundaries does not come from a place of respect or consideration for *you*. Narcissists only begin to stay on their side of the boundary because they don't want to deal with the consequence of crossing it, i.e. the pain of an electric shock.

It makes the most sense when the consequences set are proportionate to the seriousness of the ignored boundaries. The most serious violations could lead to a set time of separation, the end of the relationship, or even legal action. Lesser boundaries that are crossed may simply require a firm reminder or other smaller repercussions, such as walking to another room or leaving the house for a little

while. No matter which consequence is chosen, it will be far
easier to enforce any consequence
that has been established beforehand.

> ❧ **Growth Moment**
>
> If you have the companion
> guide to this book, the *Swimming
> with Sharks Growth Book*, take a
> moment here to check out the
> *Boundaries* Reflection Page.

What Else to Keep In Mind

Stay Factual

Stay calm and stick to the facts when having a discussion or argument with a narcissist. Emotional expressiveness will often be
turned around on you. It's much more difficult, though, for a narcissist to twist around facts. They won't be able to turn them around
on you as easily as they can with feelings or opinions.

Be Cautious of Couples and Family Therapy

Participating in couples therapy when you are in a partnership
with a narcissist can be dangerous, as can
family therapy with a parent, sibling, or other narcissistic family
member. Unless you ensure
that the couples or family
therapist is well versed in
BOTH narcissism AND
narcissistic abuse, it is possible that the therapy, and
therapist theirself, could
inadvertently do more
harm than good. Unfortu-
nately, narcissism is covered
very little in counseling pro-
grams, and narcissistic abuse even
less. Furthermore, there are very few

WARNING

COUPLES THERAPY COULD BE DANGEROUS

continuing education resources available to us. This leaves most therapists wholly unprepared to spot narcissism, let alone know how to address therapy from this perspective. Unwittingly, a well-intentioned therapist could end up further gaslighting you, encouraging you to engage in behaviors that put you at further risk, or invalidating your experiences. Asking you to open up, express your feelings, and be vulnerable can lead to further abuse and trauma. So before you engage in therapy that also includes the narcissist, make sure you do your homework AND verify with the therapist beforehand that they are well-informed in pathological narcissism and narcissistic abuse.

Narcissists Do Not
Go Down Without a Fight!

Chapter 11

SURVIVING THE HOOK

E ven when you choose the option to reel yourself out of the water to escape the shark, you're still stuck in the water for a while, because nine times out of ten, the process of leaving a narcissist is just that, a process—it doesn't happen quickly. And, because you've had to metaphorically hook yourself in order to reel yourself out, you've made yourself more vulnerable by releasing fresh blood into the water. So, when it comes to ending any sort of relationship with a narcissist, particularly one where they are your partner, one thing you can expect is for that shark to not want to let you out of the water easily.

Ending any relationship is difficult. It's natural for this process to be stressful. And it can bring out the worst in even the best people. That's just the harsh reality of one of the most painful human experiences. But ending a narcissistically abusive relationship is even worse. It will create far more than the typical emotions or reactions. Your narcissistic abuser will not be happy that you want to end the relationship, and because of this, you could experience any number of attempts to manipulate you into staying put.

The narcissist may claim that they planned to leave you anyway in an attempt to gain the upper hand. They may try to turn friends, family, colleagues, and acquaintances against you by convincing them that you are the crazy one. You could be stalked and harassed. And sadly, many narcissists at this stage will try to punish you. This could involve things like stealing money or possessions from you, lying about you, taking your pet, or trying to turn your children against you. I've seen victims have the police show up at their homes after the narcissist accused them of breaking and entering when all they did was grab their own possessions from an open garage while dropping the kids off. You might be inundated with cruel, vindictive, and threatening messages one moment which then turn "miraculously" nice if being hurtful doesn't elicit the response they want from you. The manipulation may involve fake attempts to show you they've changed (hoovering), and you could find yourself showered with attention, kind words, and gifts, much like you were at the start of your relationship (love-bombing). Although positive attention may seem enticing, it's a manipulation technique used to get you back and under their control again.

Dealing with all of this turmoil is exhausting and sometimes feels like it will never end, but it will eventually if you keep pressing forward. In the next chapters, we'll take a look at the steps you can take to prepare yourself for leaving. These will give you the tools, both in practical terms and mentally, that will set you up for the most optimal outcome. While the following information is mostly applicable to partnerships, there are parts of it that will be useful in any relationship, particularly one where there is any sort of financial or physical dependence.

Chapter 12

PREP STEP 1: RESOURCES

Whether you anticipate leaving to be a smooth process or a tumultuous one, making basic preparations is essential. If you do anticipate a tumultuous process with the potential for violent behavior to occur, your safest option is to leave secretly and without warning. If you trust that your physical safety will be ensured, then you'll still want to follow these steps for preparing to leave, but you won't necessarily need to do it under the cover of darkness, metaphorically speaking, but also potentially literally.

Bolster Up Your Support System

Leaving will be difficult no matter what, but having a support system in place will make the escape just a bit easier. Confide in people you know for sure you can trust to not go behind your back and talk to your narcissist about you. Building any support system is important right now. Additionally, finding someone who's been through narcissistic abuse can help to validate what you experience, as you experience it.

And, of course, swimming through all of this with a licensed counselor specializing in narcissistic abuse can be indispensable. Professional understanding, strict confidentiality, and access to an abundance of resources are often exactly what you need just when you need it most. Being able to confide in someone who does not have a vested interest in either side of your relationship helps you figure out what is healthy and what isn't.

Bolster Up Your Resources

If you are able to build one, a support system is a helpful resource to have, but there are several tangible resources you can prepare ahead of time that will make leaving a narcissistic partner just a little bit easier and in some cases, safer. The following is a list of resources that you will want to start gathering and hopefully have in place by the time you make you reel yourself out.

Piggy Bank

Start creating a reserve even if you're only considering leaving. That way, if you need to leave quickly, you'll be ready. You'll also need to be careful where you hide the money, whether it's cash in a physical location or a secret bank account.

Grab-&-Go Bag

Find a safe and discreet place to store the essentials you'd need in case of an immediate exit. That could include a number of basics like toiletry items and whatever else you'd pack if you were to go on vacation for several days or a week. The following are additional items to pack in your Grab-&-Go bag.

Cash

Most of us are probably used to plastic, but cash is advantageous when leaving a narcissist. It can't be tracked and there's no record of it. If your support system can afford it, consider asking them to help with this part of your transition.

Extra Keys for your House and Car

Narcissists often try to hide keys from you if they suspect something. If you have extras they don't know about, that won't be so much of a concern. Also, for those of you who have a tendency to lose your keys, you won't have to go searching for them in a panic.

Prepaid Cell Phone

Make sure you save your most important contacts on the phone right away. That way, if the narcissist grabs your main phone, or if you have to leave it behind for any other reason, you'll be able to easily reach out to your support system. Also, download any apps that may be helpful such as transportation services like Uber or Lyft. If you don't have a support system, find out the contact information and address of a local shelter and save it in your contacts and/or map.

ALENA SCIGLIANO

Pair of Clothes

Be sure to pack enough comfortable clothes in your Grab-&-Go bag to hold you over for at least a couple of days. If you know that you will still need to go to work even after leaving, include a pair of work-appropriate clothes.

Pair of Shoes

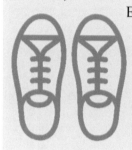

Extra shoes are an excellent idea too. Tennis shoes or sneakers would be optimal in case you are stuck walking, even a short distance. Again, if you know that you will need to go to work even after leaving, include a pair of work-appropriate shoes.

92

Chapter 13

PREP STEP 2: LEGAL COUNSEL

I t typically doesn't occur to people to consult a lawyer until after they've left the narcissist, but this can get you into unforeseen trouble. If you're dealing with someone high in malicious narcissistic traits, you're almost guaranteed an ugly and vindictive exit process. Working with a skilled, experienced, and respected lawyer is essential. Here's a list of what to consider when choosing a lawyer and navigating this process.

Note: While this advice is 100 percent applicable to those in a partnership with a narcissist and who are planning to get a divorce,

there are other relationships that might require legal guidance, particularly those that involve a vested financial interest on either side. Even if you are considering leaving a job with a narcissistic boss, or if you are the boss and need to fire an employee who is a narcissist, you might want to talk to an employment attorney to anticipate and prepare for any potential pitfalls.

For those considering divorce:

Start Saving for a Retainer

We talked earlier about your cash reserve. You may also want to set aside money or ask a family member if you can borrow a lump sum, if it's emotionally safe to do so, for your lawyer's retainer. I've seen retainers range from five to ten thousand dollars.

If you're unfamiliar with what a retainer is, basically it's a lump sum that you pay to an attorney up front, in order to reserve their services for you, and each time they bill you, the money comes from the retainer. They may request it to be replenished when it drops down to a certain amount. But these are all things to verify with the individual attorneys themselves and could easily vary based on where you are located.

Unfortunately, divorce is expensive, even when it's easy and amicable. It can get extremely costly when you're dealing with a narcissist who drags their feet and wastes everyone's time, just to get what they want or simply to make your life more difficult. And if they have access to a lot of money and know that you do not, plan to get creative, because they will take advantage of that, trying to drain your purse strings until you are helpless.

Shop Around For Your Lawyer

Even if you're not ready to leave, figure out who you'll call when you are. Ask people you know whom they might recommend. There are numerous things to consider when choosing a lawyer for this type of situation, so don't just pick the first random one that pops up from your search engine. You will potentially be working with this person for years, bare minimum will be six months to a year in most locations. Your lawyer is the person to whom you will confide your most private information. You want to feel safe and comfortable with them.

Choose a Relatable Lawyer

Find someone who understands what you're going through and can relate. Just because a lawyer meets all the legal requirements doesn't mean he or she will necessarily understand the unique challenges facing you. For this reason, consider going through a free consultation (if possible) with several lawyers to see which one best relates to your situation. Just know that sometimes, the really good ones (and probably some not-so-good ones) do charge an initial consultation fee. If you've heard great things and know that they'll meet your needs, it might be worth it though.

Choose a Lawyer Who "Gets" Pathological Narcissism

Ask the lawyer how familiar they are with pathological narcissism and narcissistic abuse. I've found that lawyers who don't understand narcissistic abuse may jump to the very wrong conclusion that you're the "mentally unstable" or "crazy" one when the underlying problem is actually the narcissistic abuse. A lawyer well-versed in pathological narcissism will fully understand your distressed emotional state given the abuse you have experienced. They will be equipped to provide compassionate help for you while knowing how to navigate interactions with the narcissist's lawyer or directly with the narcissist. Due to the nature of enduring a legal battle with a narcissist, you want someone who won't put up with the other side's manipulation tactics and will set strong boundaries.

Strategize with Your Lawyer and Know the Pitfalls

Ask your attorney to educate you on the legal process, including anything you can do to make it go better and anything you might inadvertently do that risks making it worse. Take time to strategize with your attorney to figure out what will help your case versus harm your case.

Chapter 14

PREP STEP 3: DOCUMENTATION

P art of surviving the escape is planning ahead. Many narcissists try to manipulate anyone they can to their side, including your own lawyer. They'll lie, steal, hide assets, use defamatory language against you, and more if they believe it will get them what they want. Providing factual evidence of the narcissist's abusive behavior is the most effective way to fight against this. For this reason, you will want to document literally everything. Even if you think it might not be of any use, it's better to have more than you need than not enough.

Keep in mind that the narcissist will be able to save physical evidence against you as well, so make sure that you are careful not to engage in any of the negative narcissistic abuse stress behaviors we discussed in chapter seven. These could easily be "tale twisted" and held against you.

The suggestions in this chapter are written with the idea of having evidence for court; however, I have seen where they have been helpful for victims to convince others of the abuse. Oftentimes, friends, family members, and even lawyers are incredulous as you share with them what you have gone through. One woman told me that her lawyer confided, after about a year of working for her, that she had thought the woman was "the crazy one" for months until the lawyer experienced the ex-husband's behavior firsthand. Another woman said that her parents flat-out didn't believe her until she played a recording of the narcissist.

 I recommend creating a new Google account as there are several features Google offers beyond an email address that will help you save documentation, such as Google Drive (for storing all documentation), Google Keep (quick notes like checklists, sticky notes, or voice memos), Google Docs (word documents), Google Sheets (spreadsheets).

> **💬 Growth Moment**
>
> If you have the companion guide to this book, the *Swimming with Sharks Growth Book*, take a moment here to check out the *Escape Preparation: Documentation* section.

Secret Email Accounts

You'd be surprised by how many times narcissists hack into their partner's email accounts to monitor incoming and outgoing communication as well as permanently deleting important emails. For this reason, it can be very useful having access to secret email accounts. It's okay if this feels uncomfortable. Hiding things from your partner can cause anxiety, and that is perfectly normal. Just remember that you are doing this to protect yourself (and potentially your children) from abusive behaviors and future manipulation.

Create and Forward All Documentation to a Secret Email Account

Creating a new email address with added security measures (i.e. two-step verification and security questions) is a great way to discreetly store information. To make sure that there is no record of this email address anywhere, you'll need to have the username and password memorized and not saved anywhere. Also make sure you only log into the email account from a browser that does not store history, such as Google Chrome's Incognito tabs. As you gather information, forward it all to this email address for safekeeping.

Forward Documentation to a Friend's Email Account

Ideally, you'll want this to be someone who is your friend alone and not a mutual friend, as you don't want someone to feel like they are being placed in the middle of the two of you. If you do have a friend who is comfortable with this, ask them to create a separate folder in their account where they can automatically file any of your emails for safekeeping.

Create a Record of Abuse

Document Details of Any Abusive Behavior

It's especially smart to document any abusive behavior you experience because these facts will be lied about, mischaracterized, or justified in court. And the narcissist, or their lawyer, will do anything they can to minimize or flat-out refute what you have to say. I've had patients who had to endure the opposing counsel not only grill them about traumatic abuse experiences, but also have the audacity to twist it around and blame them.

In addition to having this record as evidence, it can be helpful to read over during any moments of temptation to go back to your narcissistic abuser.

💬 If you created a new Google account, you can use Google Keep to create and store notes. It can easily be opened from within your Gmail, and is extremely easy to use and useful.

Record Interactions on Your Phone

Video can be risky, because it is more obvious. So, when possible, record using audio*. If a picture can tell a thousand words, audio can tell a hundred thousand words when it comes to how a narcissist speaks to you. Because it's difficult to predict when these situations will occur, many of my patients make it a habit to begin recording prior to the start of a conversation or interaction, just in case something happens or something is said that can be helpful to add to your record. For example, one person made sure they pressed record on their phone before every custody handoff of their child.

*Check the applicable laws wherever you live regarding recording conversations. In the US, some states allow it as long as one party knows about the recording. You would know about it, so it would be legal. But other states or countries may have different laws about it. Even if you are legally allowed to privately record conversations, if both parties do not know about it, the recordings may not be admissible in court, so check with your lawyer. Even if the recording is not admissible, there may be a workaround, such as using the recording to help you write down the details of conversations, which may be admissible. Again, verify what you can and cannot do with your lawyer!

💬 Save these recordings in Google Drive. You can organize them into folders, which will help you down the road when you need to share evidence with your lawyer, so you don't have to re-view each recording. What will be most helpful is if you create a Google Sheet that functions as an index. Title each recording, then reference it on the Google Sheet with a description of what is on the recording. You can even add a link on the sheet that will open that recording.

Save Abusive Messages/Emails/Texts

You may receive abusive emails, texts, or voice mails among other possibilities including social media messaging. Be sure to keep documentation in one centralized and secret location.

💬 Take screenshots of any of these messages and save them in a designated folder in Google Drive. Screenshots are better than copying and pasting information because they can't be altered and are less likely to be questioned.

Document Parental Negligence & Abusive Behavior

A partner very high in malignant narcissistic traits will stop at nothing to strip you of all that matters most, including your own children. They will push your emotional hot buttons and try to make you look "crazy" in front of others such as your parents or in-laws as well as during custody disputes. They will use evidence of you losing your cool in their fight to win custody of your children, even if they don't want custody, just for the sake of gaining power.

Because of their ability to deceive, you'll want to document any of their abusive behavior or parental negligence. The last thing you want to encounter is a court date without documented facts because that's where narcissists thrive best. They will manipulate and sway the emotions of others, and they'll often hire lawyers who are skilled in the same way. If your kids come home from the narcissist's custody talking about how they were treated poorly or neglected (physically or emotionally), make sure you discreetly record your child saying these things. If you are unable to press record on your phone in time, intentionally make notes in Google Keep or Google Docs as soon as you can to avoid forgetting or mixing up any details. If your children's teachers begin mentioning that they are seeing a pattern of certain negative behaviors occurring after they were in the narcissist's custody, ask them if they would be willing to keep a record of what they notice.

Remember, narcissists are master manipulators. They will use this skill to its fullest when facing any sort of legal battle with you. Having lots of documentation to support your case can only help you. Even if the narcissist tries to deny or lie about what they've done, sticking to the facts, especially if they are documented, will make the process far less stressful for you and far more difficult for them to manipulate.

Chapter 15

PREP STEP 4: SELF-CARE

One of the side effects of being in a relationship with a narcissist is that your life revolves around them and their needs. As you are preparing for your escape, you'll benefit from learning or relearning the skill of self-care and nurturing your own needs. There are many ways to provide yourself self-care, such as engaging in one of your hobbies, spending time with friends, exercising, spending time outdoors, and reading an enjoyable book, among others. If you struggle coming up with ideas, try searching online for some suggestions. As far as therapeutic self-care options are concerned, two of the best are journaling and therapy, which I'll discuss here.

Therapeutic Journaling

Whereas documenting involves recording the facts or truth of what happens as it unfolds, journaling allows you an important outlet to process the emotions you experience while in a narcissistically abusive relationship (and while leaving it). The primary benefit of your journal is its therapeutic value. You can voice your frustrations and point of view without being bullied, belittled, or discounted. You're able to start realizing again that you can trust your judgment despite what you've been told by your abuser. This is also your opportunity to get angry or cry on the page without being told you're overreacting or crazy. It provides a safe place to process your emotions in a healthy way.

The only caveat is that you need to make sure your partner can't access your journal. For that reason, consider storing your journal in a safe place or on a secure app on your phone. *Normally, I share with patients that it tends to be more therapeutic to handwrite their journal; however, if this means risking further abuse, opt for the secure app on your phone.*

💭 Google Docs can also be a great place to journal.

Seek Individual Therapy

Individual therapy is crucial during this vulnerable time as you'll have a myriad of decisions to make and emotions to work through. Once you are ready, therapy will help you gain a better understanding of how to rebuild your sense of self-worth. You'll also learn how to trust your intuition again and gain greater insight into the playbook narcissists use.

Counselors who specialize in narcissistic abuse are hard to come by. If you don't have one within driving distance, whom you can see in person, don't hesitate to reach out to someone else who can provide teletherapy. Just know that typically, but not always, therapists are required to be licensed in the state in which you are located. So, take that into consideration as you search.

If it really becomes difficult to find someone who has availability within your state, double-check your state laws regarding licensing requirements for professional counselors. There is a fantastic app that makes this easy, called "Telemental Health Laws," compiled by the law firm, Epstein Becker Green, P.C.

Find a Therapist for your Children

The combined pain of years of narcissistic abuse coupled with the need to leave the relationship can feel beyond overwhelming. You'll often feel like all you can do is just survive. Because of your own pain, you may not realize how badly your children are suffering. Or, you may be reading into your child's behavior more than necessary and thinking that they are struggling more than they really are. Each child will process the family distress in their own way. And since they'll have far fewer facts and understanding than you do, it could feel all the more confusing, frustrating, terrifying, and angering.

Because of this, I strongly suggest that you consider seeking a therapist who specializes in working with children. Not only will this help you sort through and better understand what exactly your child is experiencing, this will also help your child work through the many challenges they'll face with less confusion. It will speed up their soul-mending too!

Finding the Right Therapist

One thing I tell the therapists in my group practice is that they can either be good at a bunch of different specialties or they can be fantastic at a couple. As you search for therapists, pay attention to what they say they specialize in. If you see a long list of items, there is a good chance that they are only good at each of them. But when it comes to working through the narcissistic abuse stress you've endured, you want to work with someone who is going to be great at that one thing. Similarly, if you are looking for a counselor for your child, look for someone who specializes in treating children and is certified in play therapy. A therapist who claims to work with ages four to eighty-four is either very inexperienced and is trying to see whomever they can in order to acquire the necessary hours for licensure, or they aren't focused enough on fine-tuning the skills that are required to successfully provide therapy to children. I'm sure that there are exceptions out there, but unless your choices are very limited, opt for a therapist who clinically focuses on your needs so that you can receive the best treatment possible. If you are faced with limited options and none that include specialties in NAb, try to find someone who at least specializes in trauma. Then, consider asking any therapist you talk to if they would be willing to read this or another book that resonates with you on narcissistic abuse. At least you'll know that you are both on the same page regarding your level of knowledge about narcissistic abuse.

Another thing to keep in mind when searching for the right therapist is that you want to find the right one for *you*. Similarly to how we don't mesh with every person we come across in our daily lives, you are not going to mesh with every counselor just because they are a counselor. If you don't feel a connection within the first or second session, don't hesitate to try someone else. This isn't like finding a doctor for your annual physicals or a mechanic to change the oil in your car. You'll be spending far more time with this person. Your therapist will likely be the one person to whom you bare more of your soul than anyone else in your life. Particularly

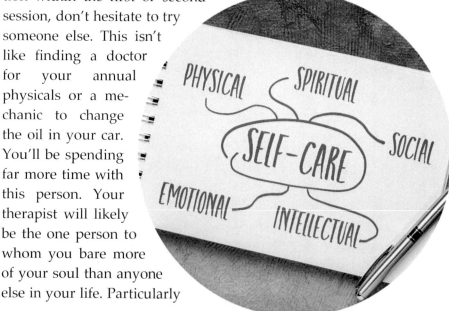

when recovering from narcissistic abuse, you need someone with whom you can feel safe being vulnerable. I know that you are anxious to mend your soul and feel better, but this is a long journey. Have patience and take the time you need to find just the right therapist for you!

Chapter 16

PARENTING ALONGSIDE
A NARCISSIST

There is a reason why I didn't title this chapter "Parenting *With* a Narcissist." Whether you are still together or have already separated, parenting with a narcissist just doesn't happen and parenting alongside a narcissist is still extremely difficult. Based on your particular situation and the type of narcissist, there are many influencing factors that impact the difficulties you may be facing or may have yet to face. This is another reason why seeking individual counseling is important. A counselor can help you work through the emotions that surface as well as determine your best courses of action to maintain peace and raise your children in as healthy a way as possible.

Healthy vs. Unhealthy Modeling

One of the unfortunate realities of having children with a narcissist is knowing the impact that the narcissist has on your children. You witness how they mistreat or neglect your children but feel powerless to fix it. You see the unhealthy behaviors that the narcissist models to your child but can't prevent your child from seeing them too. So what are your options in a situation with so little control? You only have control over your own choices right now, so make sure you are making the healthiest ones possible.

Even though your child may be witnessing their other parent make unhealthy choices, you can make up for that. It may not always seem like that's possible, but I promise, you will be able to make a difference. Worst case scenario, you are planting seeds that your child can nurture and grow in the future. Best case scenario, your child will be drawn to and encouraged by your healthy behavior now, which will lead them to strive to behave similarly throughout childhood and as they grow into adulthood.

Is It Love or Fear?

What's the best way to model healthy behavior? Focus on love versus fear! Allow love to guide your choices and behaviors, rather than fear. Intentionally guide yourself through this simple process by asking yourself either of the following two questions:

Is my reaction rooted in love or fear?
OR
Would this choice be rooted in love or fear?

When you allow love to guide your mind over fear, you cannot make the wrong choice. The tricky part is being honest with yourself in identifying when fear has guided you rather than love. Fear has a sneaky way of masking itself for love, especially when it comes to relationships. You may even be thinking, "Alena, you are way off. I'm in this position in the first place because of love, because I chose to love this person who ended up being a narcissist!" I can see where you might think that, but I would argue that if you look closely enough and really examine what led you to stay in that unhealthy relationship, you would be able to see that it was fear, not love.

Is It Love or Fear?

So as you go through your day, trying to model the healthiest behaviors possible to your children, just remember to check in with yourself to make sure that you are intentionally coming from a place of love. If you're upset at your kid for something and tempted to yell at them, remind yourself that yelling comes from a place of fear, not love. If you receive a text message from your ex and feel wound up and anxious, check in with yourself by asking if that reaction is rooted in love or fear. The answer will most certainly be fear, and identifying that now gives you the opportunity to ask yourself what your reaction would be if it were coming from a place of love. Keep in mind that a decision rooted in love won't always be about someone else. Oftentimes, your answer lies in the place that is loving toward yourself.

> **Growth Moment**
>
> If you have the companion guide to this book, the *Swimming with Sharks Growth Book*, take a moment here to check out the *Is It Love or Fear?* reflection page.

Shared Custody and Co-Parenting vs. Parallel Parenting

One of the greatest concerns victims of narcissistic abuse bring into therapy is how to "co-parent" with a narcissist. Here's the thing though, if you've separated from the narcissist, and you are raising your child in separate households, co-parenting rarely ends up being a viable or effective course of action. When it comes to a narcissist and non-narcissist trying to raise a child separately, your best bet is to plan on parallel parenting. Parallel parenting is actually a great example of a healthy boundary to set with a narcissist. While it may seem like parallel parenting would give you less control over how the narcissist is parenting your child, the reality is that you wouldn't have had any control anyway within a co-parenting situation. Co-parenting requires too much cooperation from the narcissist to ever work, so you will end up feeling like you're either banging your head against a wall, repeatedly disappointed by the narcissist, or living in a state of fear of what the narcissist will do or say next with regard to your own parenting. Opting instead for parallel parenting frees you of your expectation that the other parent will cooperate. It also allows you to parent without interference from the narcissist and in the way that you best see fit. So in return for giving up the illusion of control that co-parenting offers, you've gained more autonomy and will be able to better maintain your sanity and your own relationship with your child. Furthermore, if neither of you are trying to coordinate your parenting, your fear will be triggered less, and you will be able to live from a place of love more. Imagine what life will be like without all of that unnecessary anxiety!

Please note that it is not uncommon for the legal system to "impose" co-parenting on parents who are going through a custody battle by requiring them to participate together in co-parenting courses, co-parenting counseling, or participation in regular meetings with a co-parenting coordinator. Talk with your lawyer about this ahead of time and make sure you are both prepared to make a case to the judge for parallel parenting. You'll need to explain how forcing you into a co-parenting dynamic would be harmful to you and likely lead to further abuse, in addition to how the children are negatively impacted by the arguments and futile attempts at co-parenting. If necessary, ask your lawyer to point out that you would not be required to spend time with a partner who had physically abused you, risking further physical abuse, so you should not be forced to spend time with someone who has psychologically abused you, creating an opportunity for continued psychological abuse.

Frequently Asked Parenting Questions

Will my child become a narcissist?

There is no clear-cut answer to this, but I will say that your child's other parent being a narcissist does not mean that your child will automatically become a narcissist as well. You'll see in the following section of the book, when we discuss the nature of narcissists, that children of narcissists are at greater risk of developing narcissistic traits, but I believe that you can help prevent this from occurring.

There are three parts to effectively nurturing a child away from narcissistic tendencies:

1. Help them develop a healthy self-image that is able to learn from guilt rather than internalize it as shame.
2. Teach them how to have compassion and empathize with others, and make sure they actively use that skill on a regular basis.
3. Develop their social awareness.

Having a healthy level of self-esteem that is not easily threatened or prone to shame will ensure that your child does not adopt the traits that narcissists use to avoid shame. Additionally, being able to recognize how their actions impact another person through strong social awareness, along with readily empathizing with that person, will ensure that your child doesn't develop the tactics narcissists use to control others, also a means to avoid their own shame.

How do I protect my child from the narcissist when we have shared custody?

As a parent, it's your job to put the narcissist's behavior into context, so the behavior doesn't fully shape the child's worldview. Notice that I referred to "the behavior," not "the narcissist." This is because focusing on unhealthy behavior is much more constructive and limits the risk of being accused of parental alienation. It will also help to maintain whatever positive relationship your child does have with the narcissistic parent while also ensuring that they do not grow up believing that it's okay to be treated as they have been by their narcissistic parent. As you address this with your child, tread carefully. You won't want to speak judgmentally about the other parent. Not only could that come back to hurt you in any future legal battles for custody, it could also damage your child's relationship with their other parent in an unhealthy way. At the same time, you want to be realistic and honest with your child to help guide them in what is healthy versus unhealthy.

This is another circumstance in which you can use love vs. fear as your guiding principle. If you are coming from a place of love when engaging in these types of conversations with your child, then you won't end up speaking about the other parent in a judgmental and critical way. Your tone will be factual and objective while also focusing on the child's experience and understanding of the behavior.

Under other circumstances, I would make very different recommendations regarding child-rearing. However, when it comes to raising a child alongside a narcissist, you are going to need to teach your child how to survive without letting them know that's what you're actually doing. The following are some examples of how to go about this:

> Teach them resilience and coping skills that will help them to withstand potential narcissistic trauma.

> Teach them what healthy boundaries are, while at the same time explaining that to maintain peace with their other parent, they may not be able to maintain or enforce those boundaries all the time. If they can at least know what healthy boundaries ought to be, then they'll know how to implement them in other relationships.

> Teach them how to mentally compartmentalize so that they can successfully function whenever they are not with you.

> Provide the child with the emotional space that will permit them to break down and express their full range of emotions. They will need to be able to do this while they are with you, since they won't be able to at the other parent's home.

Once a child is old enough, usually at some point during their teenage years, it will be appropriate to be more open and direct with them. Telling your teenager that how they are being treated by their other parent is unhealthy and unacceptable can be validating, healing, and empowering. Just remember to emphasize that you are not saying that their other parent is bad, only that their behaviors are unhealthy, and if you believe it is an appropriate time to do so, you could even explain that certain behaviors are abusive. This is not only your chance to teach your child how to survive within their relationship with their narcissistic parent, it is your opportunity to teach them what unhealthy relationships look like for when they are an adult. Without understanding the differences between unhealthy and healthy relationship dynamics, your child is more likely to be drawn into relationships with narcissists in adulthood. I'll explain more with regard to this in the next part of the book.

*Please note: Don't label the other parent as a "narcissist" to your child. Instead, focus on labeling the behaviors as described earlier in the book.

What do I say to my child when they are hurt by their narcissistic parent?

- ➤ Validate how your child experiences their other parent's behavior.
- ➤ Share with them that they aren't wrong to be hurt by what their other parent does.
- ➤ Let them know that their other parent is loving them as best as they can, but that they don't always know how to show it in healthy ways.
- ➤ Explain that sometimes the other parent becomes overwhelmed by their own fear and shame, which prevents them from behaving in loving ways, as the child deserves.

➢ Tell your child that they are loved no matter what and that you will always love them unconditionally. This is important in order to compensate for the conditional love they may be experiencing with the other parent.

Part Four

THE NATURE
OF NARCISSISTS

Whether you are still treading water while staying in your relationship with the narcissist, or you have decided to reel yourself out and begin the process of leaving the narcissist behind, like everyone I have worked with, you are probably becoming anxious to have a deeper understanding of what makes the narcissist tick. I'm sure you've been wondering why they are the way they are and how they became that way. As humans, we struggle to accept things that don't make sense. And the behavior of narcissists is one thing that tends to make the least sense in life. It's hard to grasp how anyone would choose to treat another person in such an abusive way, especially when we think they are someone who loves us. So it's unsurprising that you would be ready to scour through any information you can get your hands on in order to try to make sense of the nonsensical.

Furthermore, things that don't make sense create a feeling of helplessness, which leaves us feeling like we aren't in control. When we don't feel in control, fear kicks in. While fear of a certain threat is a healthy instinctual emotion that is meant to protect us from harm and keep us alive, it can also warp itself into unproductive anxiety over an uncertain threat, which inevitably becomes unhealthy. So how do we gain back a sense of control and drive out the fear and anxiety? Knowledge. Knowledge is the key to driving out fear, because increasing our knowledge helps us to make sense of what is going on around us, which then helps us to feel like we are back in control.

In Part Four, as we're trying to gain a better understanding of the nature of narcissists, we'll explore empathy, what true narcissism really is, pathological narcissism, types of narcissists, how shame and power relate to narcissists, narcissistic supply, and narcissistic parents.

Chapter 17

WHAT IS EMPATHY?

To understand pathological narcissism, you first need to truly understand empathy. Some of you may be well-versed in empathy; however, I am sure there are many of you who do not truly understand what empathy really is. I didn't. I honestly do not remember anyone ever using this word prior to my graduate program, where we were taught about empathy because it is probably the single most important part of counseling. The word sympathy is frequently used, but it lacks the power that empathy possesses. Sympathy is often likened to feeling and expressing pity or compassion for a hardship that someone else is experiencing. Whereas empathy can be experienced regardless of the circumstance or feeling. Empathy is the act of trying to understand someone else's emotional experience, by putting yourself in their position and trying to see things from their point of view. For some people, it may begin from a cognitive place but then transform into an emotional and visceral experience. For example, if you come across someone whose sister just died, you may end up feeling a physical ache in your chest, as you empathize with them. Empathy is tapping into similar emotions you've experienced but under different circumstances.

While feelings are universal, situations and circumstances are not. However, you do not need to have experienced the same situation in order to empathize with someone. Sometimes, you may not have experienced anything in your life that is remotely similar, but you can do your best to imagine what the emotional experience of someone else might be. When it comes to thoughts, ideas, and opinions, you may have a completely different point of view, but by putting yourself in the other person's shoes, you can understand their perspective by tapping into similar emotions that underlie their perspective.

Empathy is powerful and can be transformative. It allows people to connect with one another on a deeper level. The one on the receiving end of empathy feels heard, understood, and accepted. It is probably the most underutilized skill in the world, and yet a simple expression of empathy has the power to de-escalate rising tensions, resolve conflict, and foster peace, whether on a micro or macro level. On the other hand, a deficit of empathy not only breeds conflict and tension, but it inhibits the ability to heal. This is one reason why a deficit of empathy is so problematic for people in relationships with narcissists. It's difficult to truly accept, heal, and move on after you've been hurt, when the person who hurt you did not show empathy for your pain.

Empathic Failures

Empathic failures occur when there is a lack of understanding of another person's feelings, perceptions, and thoughts. This can occur when someone tries to show empathy but misses the mark completely, or when someone neglects to express empathy at all. It also happens when your emotional experience is invalidated, or someone tells you that you have no right to feel a certain way.

Empathy Atypical

Have you heard of the terms neurotypical and neuroatypical? You might have come across a person with autism being described as neuroatypical. I thought it would be apt to apply the "-typical" and "-atypical" suffixes to the term empathy as well. While most of us would be considered empathy-typical, a narcissist is most certainly empathy-atypical. Their ability to empathize with others is severely underdeveloped.

The narcissist's empathy-atypical nature underlies the majority of their dysfunctional behavior. Because they lack the level of empathy needed to regulate their choices, their actions tend to be borne out of a complete lack of consideration of how they might affect other people. This is how a narcissist is able to treat others in narcissistically abusive ways. Since they aren't trying to imagine how their behavior might make the other person feel, it doesn't occur to them to reconsider or stop what they are doing. While being empathy-atypical doesn't cause a narcissist to behave the way they do, it does lead to the lack of checks and balances that empathy-typical people have, which otherwise helps to ensure behavior regulation.

Chapter 18

WHAT IS A NARCISSIST?

T he explanation to this question is both simple and complicated. In fact, this was one of the more difficult chapters for me to write, going through numerous revisions and complete overhauls in order to explain it in just the right way. But what I realized is that it needs to be explained in both ways, the simple and the complicated. The complicated explanation of what a narcissist is requires a discussion of what healthy narcissism and pathological narcissism are, what causes someone to develop pathological narcissism, breaking down what personality is, as well as the subconscious and conscious ways that personality plays a role in what makes someone a narcissist—all of which we will cover later in this chapter. There is not one distinct linear way to explain each of these though, so if you're finding one part confusing because you need to understand another part first, feel free to skip around in this chapter.

Firstly, let's address two fundamental terms, *pathological* and *personality*, that are commonly used when discussing narcissism and narcissists to make sure we're all on the same page.

Pathological (adjective):

1. : when someone's behavior is to such a degree that is extreme, excessive, markedly abnormal, or unacceptable

2. : caused by or evidencing a mentally disturbed condition

Personality comprises how an individual thinks, feels, and behaves, and is shaped by their experiences, environment, and genetics.

☞ **Personality** = how we think, feel, and behave

☞ **Personality** is shaped by our:

◆ *Experiences*: such as how we were treated as children

◆ *Environment*: such as how we were raised (safe and loving environment vs. insecure and fear-based environment)

◆ *Inherited Characteristics*: such as genetic factors that predispose us to be more empathic vs. less empathic, more socially aware vs. less socially aware

A **narcissist** can most simply be explained as someone who is:

☞ Deeply Insecure ➡ False Self-Image created

☞ Overcompensates (for their insecurity and to support the false self-image) ➡ Grandiose Behaviors

☞ Overreacts (to anything that triggers the insecurity or threatens to shatter the false self-image) ➡ Narcissistically Abusive Behaviors

A narcissist, by the way, is aware of none of these. While the narcissist's insecurity isn't visible from the outside, the other two characteristics, overcompensation and overreaction, are what we do see and are key to identifying someone as a narcissist.

Let's expand a little on our explanation of what a narcissist is.

☞ Deeply **insecure** because they have a **distorted self-image** that creates a **subconscious** but debilitating **fear** of not being good enough (**shame**), the feeling of which is avoided at all costs.

☞ As a result, their brain interprets anything that may trigger shame as a **threat** to their existence.

☞ This led to the development of a **pathological level of narcissism**—an extreme focus on the self, which functions as a **survival** mechanism.

☞ Part of this includes **defense mechanisms** that enable the narcissist to avoid looking within and seeing theirself as not good enough—experiencing shame.

　◆ One of the primary defense mechanisms is the creation of a **false self-image**, an image of how a narcissist wants to see theirself and how they want others to see them.

☞ The other part includes **offensive tactics** to enable them to push away anyone they perceive as a threat to their avoidance of shame.

☞ The **defense mechanisms** and **offensive tactics** manifest as **narcissistic abuse**.

☞ Due to **deficient levels of empathy and compassion** as well as **poor social awareness**, they do not anticipate that their behaviors will hurt others or recognize them as abusive.

Here's the kicker though. Their self-awareness stinks too, so they have zero awareness of any of the above.

To summarize, a narcissist has a **distorted self-image** and is deeply **insecure** which leads to **fear** and avoidance of **shame**. To cope, a person develops a **pathological level of narcissism** which includes **defense mechanisms** and **offensive tactics**. One of the primary defense mechanisms is the creation of a **false self-image** which the narcissist does their best to maintain, both for theirself and for others. When these factors are combined with a **deficient level of compassion and empathy** development as well as **poor social awareness**, then as an adult, the narcissist is unable to identify when their attempts to maintain their false self-image will lead to behaviors that take advantage of or harm another person. The combination of each of these factors translates into **narcissistic abuse**.

Why Does Someone Become a Narcissist?

To understand this we'll need to discuss narcissism, pathological narcissism, what causes someone to have a pathological level of narcissism, and how this shapes their personality. Please keep in mind that first of all, no one has identified just one specific thing that causes someone to be a narcissist. Second of all, my explanations below are a synthesis of several different theories in the field of psychology that have countless books and scientific articles written on each one. I most certainly have left out details that another mental health professional may think would have been essential to include. Third of all, I am speaking from my own experience as a licensed clinician, what I have learned, and the data I have gathered from my patients, as well as the research I have done over the past ten years, reviewing the work of other professionals. This may be an incomplete picture, but it is the most complete one I could describe in the confines of a chapter.

"How did he even

become a narcissist?"

—Anonymous patient

married to a narcissist

What Is Narcissism?

If you do a search online, many of the answers you find to the question, "What is narcissism," will say something to the effect of narcissism being an unhealthy admiration and preoccupation with oneself. Not only do I think this answer is oversimplified, it's not completely correct. The desire to understand and explain excessive self-admiration is as old as Greek mythology. Narcissus, whose name is the origin of the modern term, fell in love with his own reflection in a pool of water. Because he became so obsessed and literally could not stop admiring his image, he eventually died from the wasting away of his body. Evolving from one theorist to another, the term narcissism in psychology was introduced by early psychoanalytic theorists.

The Narcissism Spectrum

The other part of the answer that your search engine doesn't give you is that narcissism is present in all of us. Put simply, **narcissism is a focus on self**. As human beings, we experience narcissism on a **spectrum, with a healthy level of narcissism on one end and an unhealthy level present on the other end.** Since we're all self-focused to a certain extent, we all fall somewhere on the spectrum of narcissism. Some hardly focus on themselves at all, while others are self-focused to a pathological level that interferes with their daily life and interpersonal relationships. Teenagers and children are naturally more narcissistic. Without a developmentally healthy level of narcissism, they wouldn't be able to create their own identity or develop into independent, well-functioning adults. Furthermore, we all need a certain amount of narcissism for self-preservation. **Without being able to focus inward, we would struggle to find balance between the giving of ourselves to others and preserving enough of ourselves for self-care.** Keeping your own interests in mind is also crucial to prevent you and those closest to you from being exploited, poorly treated, or even harmed. As you can see, setting these "self-centric" boundaries can be healthy for both you and others in your life.

Narcissism Spectrum

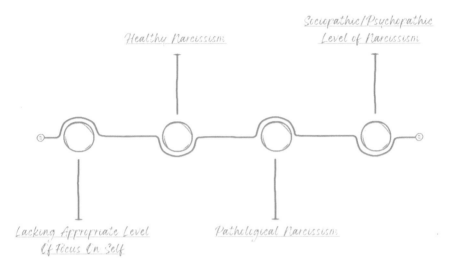

Healthy Narcissism

Sociopathic/Psychopathic Level of Narcissism

Lacking Appropriate Level Of Focus On Self

Pathological Narcissism

(Narcissism = Focus On Self)

Pathological Narcissism

As we defined it earlier in this chapter, using the descriptor, *pathological*, indicates that someone's behavior is extreme, excessive, markedly abnormal, unacceptable, and caused by or evidence of a mentally disturbed condition. The unhealthy end of the narcissism spectrum is indeed pathological because it is an extreme, excessive, abnormal, and unacceptable focus on self. Furthermore, this, in itself, is what causes a mentally disturbed condition. And while **"mentally disturbed"** sounds pretty strong, we're going to take it at face value and recognize that it refers to a **disruption to the normal pattern or function of someone's mental state**.

So the normal functioning of someone's mental state would include a healthy level of narcissism—a healthy amount of self-focus for the sake of self-preservation and a balance of giving of oneself with self-care. Whereas pathological narcissism causes a dysfunctional focus on the self leading to personality patterns that are destructive to both the individual and those around them.

What Causes Someone to Have a Pathological Level of Narcissism?

In my explanation of what a narcissist is, I briefly mentioned that pathological narcissism is developed as a protective and survival mechanism against any perceived threats that might cause a narcissist to experience shame. I also mentioned that this fear of shame comes from a distorted self-image. But what causes someone to develop a distorted self-image in the first place?

☞ When a child grows up with a parent or caregiver who repeatedly commits empathic failures, failing to understand or acknowledge the child's thoughts, feelings, and perceptions, the child feels wounded over and over again. While repeated empathic failures of parents or caregivers is a potential indicator that they are a narcissist, regardless of what the cause of the empathic failures may be, the bottom line is that the child's emotional needs are not met. This creates a dynamic in which a child may not develop a healthy attachment to that parent or caregiver.

☞ It is through our relationship and attachment to our parents that we grow to understand ourselves and the world around us. A child is meant to develop a healthy attachment to their parent or caregiver so that they can develop a healthy sense of self, or self-image. Without this, a person's inner self isn't afforded the opportunity to develop in a healthy way.

☞ If there is abuse or repeated empathic failures by a parent or caregiver, and a child's development of healthy attachment is disrupted, they are left with an underdeveloped sense of self, creating a very fragile and distorted self-image.

☞ It is this distorted self-image that establishes an underlying vulnerability and insecurity which gives rise to numerous potentially unhealthy patterns of self-protective behavior, including pathological narcissism.

This explains why the survivor-victim patients I have worked with repeatedly identify that at least one parent of the narcissist in their life was also a narcissist.

Understanding the Fragility and Defense System of a Narcissist

Sometimes, the best way for us to move forward is to deepen our understanding of someone else's existence. And sometimes the best way to do that is to relate to them through the use of an analogy. When helping my patients gain a deeper understanding of what it means to be a narcissist, I like to use the analogy of a glass orb. You know those crackled-glass orbs that are commonly used for decoration? They appear to be vulnerable to shattering at the slightest touch. Imagine you have a precious crackled-glass orb that someone very special gave to you, and you can't imagine how horrible you would feel if it broke. You know that you can't just store it on a high shelf, away from the grasp of anyone who enters your house. That's not safe enough. You have to carry it around with you wherever you go, every single day, increasing its vulnerability. To help protect it, you decide to wrap it in a layer of bubble wrap. But you realize that just one layer won't do the trick, so you add another layer, and then another layer, and so on. Even though you now have these layers of protection, if there is even the slightest hint that someone might get close enough to crush the orb by bumping into it or sitting on it, you lash out, yelling at them to stay away. Now, you've not only developed a defense system of bubble wrap, you've also developed an offensive tactic of scaring people away.

A person who has a distorted self-image subconsciously feels at great risk of shattering and not being able to pick up their own pieces, which to them is a threat to their very existence. This is the inner experience of a pathological narcissist. Because it happens subconsciously, they are not aware that they hold onto a fear that at any moment the glass orb they are protecting within theirself might shatter. So they develop defense mechanisms and offensive tactics to protect against that happening. Essentially, the unhealthy narcissistic behaviors they develop are simply ways of protecting themselves from shattering. They've metaphorically wrapped themselves in bubble wrap (charm, charisma, power, prestige, etc.). When someone gets too close though, perhaps by challenging or questioning them, this is interpreted as a threat and leads them to implement their offensive tactics, lashing out and pushing the person away, thus mitigating the risk of the orb shattering.

Keep in mind that just because you have a better understanding of the narcissist, that doesn't mean you will be any better equipped to change them. I share these concepts with you so that you can more easily accept them for who they are, including the fact that you don't have the power to change them or inspire them to choose to change. This is for your sake, not theirs. I want you to be able to live your life free of the perpetual false hope that they can change. The sooner you accept that, the sooner you will be able to live in peace and mend your soul.

What's the Difference Between a Narcissist and a Pathological Narcissist?

Nothing, really. Referring to someone as a narcissist has an inherent implication of pathological narcissism; however, I often prefer to include the modifier, opting for the term "pathological narcissist" to make it absolutely clear that we are talking about someone whose behavior is unacceptable and evidence of being mentally disturbed. When brevity is called for though, I will use them interchangeably.

Misconceptions about Diagnosing

Using the term "narcissist" or "pathological narcissist" does not specify whether or not someone qualifies for a diagnosable condition such as Narcissistic Personality Disorder, and I want to reiterate and be very clear that **calling someone a narcissist or pathological narcissist is not assigning a diagnosis to them**. Referring to someone as a narcissist is similar to referring to someone as a perfectionist. You are simply describing an aspect of who they are. One which happens to influence their personality and in the case of a narcissist, is quite harmful to others. On that note, it's also important to remember that this is only one part of who a person is. Every human being has many dimensions. And recognizing that someone is a pathological narcissist does not necessarily mean that they are entirely a *bad* person, just that they treat certain other people in hurtful ways due to *bad* choices. It is these bad choices that are the reason why staying away from or setting impenetrable boundaries is the healthiest way to handle a narcissist.

Narcissistic Personality Disorder

Concerns Related to Everyday Usage of the Term "Narcissistic Personality Disorder"

Before I get into defining Narcissistic Personality Disorder, I want to share some notes that I think are important for everyone to know. First of all, attaching a *personality disorder* label to someone carries a very heavy weight with it and isn't to be taken lightly. To consider someone as having a personality disorder is to imply that the pieces that make up their personality, their thoughts, feelings, and behavior, function differently than what one would expect within their culture, *and* it causes problems over a long period of time within interpersonal and/or intrapersonal aspects of their life, *and* because our personalities tend to stay the same over time, those who have personality disorders very rarely change over the course of their lifetime.

Second of all, not only does someone need to be a qualified mental health professional to diagnose anyone with a mental disorder, but in the counseling profession, it is unethical to diagnose someone without assessing them directly. The conundrum is that narcissists rarely present themselves in the office of a licensed counselor or psychologist in order to be assessed. They seldom seek out therapy for themselves, and on the rare occasion that narcissists do attend therapy, it is usually for factors they see as external to themselves, such as frustrations with a boss or when a partner insists on couples therapy. When they do go to therapy, the very nature of the disorder makes it extremely difficult for even experienced clinicians to identify right away, if at all.

It is for these reasons that I find it more appropriate to use the term "pathological narcissist," leaving out any reference to a personality disorder. It's also just not necessary to say that someone has the disorder. "Pathological narcissist" is sufficient in making it clear that someone not only focuses on theirself to an unhealthy level but that they do it to an extreme extent which negatively impacts others. Admittedly, it's a bit redundant since the term "narcissist" already implies a pathology. Considering the vast harm that is inflicted on the innocent by narcissists, though, I figure it's appropriate to make it abundantly clear that the nature of this condition is harmful and, honestly, dangerous to those in their life, just like a shark. So, we'll tack on "pathological" for good measure and continue referring to them as "pathological narcissists."

> ### A note to fellow therapists:
> As someone who focuses primarily on psychotherapy and does not conduct formal psychological assessments, I have found two reliable ways to detect if someone *might* be a narcissist. If they are your patient, it can become clear by reflecting on your own countertransference, the emotional reaction we have to our patients. I have also found that the most efficient way to determine if someone is a narcissist is by talking with their family members or close friends. Patterns of interpersonal communication and how members of a narcissist's life experience them are the greatest telltale signs of pathological narcissism.

Defining Narcissistic Personality Disorder

Narcissistic Personality Disorder, or NPD, is only considered if a person possesses or exhibits a minimum number of narcissistic traits, and those traits interfere with the individual's daily functioning. This criteria is based on the traits recognized in the Diagnostic and Statistical Manual of Mental Disorders, Fifth Edition (DSM-5). The problem is that the DSM-5 includes traits that are mainly associated with grandiose narcissists, leaving out the other narcissist populations.

Knowing that this is not a comprehensive view of what is often seen in narcissistic personalities, let's still look at how the DSM-5 characterizes NPD. The DSM-5 recognizes nine traits regularly present in individuals with Narcissistic Personality Disorder. At least five of these must consistently occur, and interfere with the individual's daily functioning, typically interpersonal relationships, for someone to receive an NPD diagnosis. Here is exactly what it says:

> A pervasive pattern of grandiosity (in fantasy or behavior), need for admiration, and lack of empathy, beginning by early adulthood and present in a variety of context, as indicated by five (or more) of the following:
>
> 1. Has a grandiose sense of self-importance (e.g., exaggerates achievements and talents, expects to be recognized as superior without commensurate achievements).
>
> 2. Is preoccupied with fantasies of unlimited success, power, brilliance, beauty, or ideal love.
>
> 3. Believes that he or she is "special" and unique and can only be understood by, or should associate with, other special or high-status people (or institutions).
>
> 4. Requires excessive admiration.
>
> 5. Has a sense of entitlement (i.e., unreasonable expectations of especially favorable treatment or automatic compliance with his or her expectations).
>
> 6. Is interpersonally exploitative (i.e., takes advantage of others to achieve his or her own ends).
>
> 7. Lacks empathy, is unwilling to recognize or identify with the feelings and needs of others.
>
> 8. Is often envious of others or believes that others are envious of him or her.
>
> 9. Shows arrogant, haughty behavior or attitudes.

Having shared the diagnostic criteria, it's important to reiterate that one must be professionally qualified to diagnose someone with NPD. Only qualified mental health clinicians trained in Narcissistic Personality Disorder, who have properly evaluated the individual, can make this determination.

As you can see, many of the descriptors listed above only apply to some of the narcissists out there. This is because when this diagnosis was developed, it focused solely on the grandiose/overt type of narcissist, and it has not been updated yet to include the criteria for covert narcissists. (We'll get into types of narcissists in the next chapter.)

In addition to the diagnosis lacking coverage of the full picture of pathological narcissism, another concern related to the presence of this diagnosis in the DSM-5 is that attaching the diagnosis to someone provides them the opportunity to take advantage of being diagnosed with a mental disorder. Because many narcissists feel entitled and often use exploitation to get what they want, they may exploit the diagnosis to receive accommodations or services that are not warranted but that others may be legally required to provide.

Chapter 19

SHARK SPECIES: TYPES OF NARCISSISTS

Just as the great white isn't the only species of shark in the ocean, there isn't just one type of narcissist. However, I generally don't find it to be clinically useful to categorize narcissists, so I'll provide only a brief introduction to the labels I do use. If this interests you, it may be worthwhile doing some research online where you can find a plethora of information on the various labels that have been created to describe different variations of narcissists. However, keep in mind that not everything you read about narcissism is accurate. Many articles quote professionals as though they are experts in the field of narcissism or narcissistic abuse, and yet there is no evidence of that on their websites or professional profiles, which may explain why there is a significant amount of misinformation out there.

For example, I recently got frustrated reading an article online that attempted to delineate the various types of narcissists. It claimed that "vulnerable narcissism" is characterized by insecurity, low self-esteem, and hypersensitivity. Here's the thing though, EVERY narcissist, no matter the type, is insecure, has low self-esteem, and is hypersensitive. My best guess for why there is a desire to split up narcissists into categories is because they can be difficult to understand which, understandably so, can cause anxiety. Being able to narrow down the type of narcissist they are to one specific label can feel comforting because it allows you to feel a greater sense of control.

Some of the terms listed are ones that I use occasionally in my work with survivor victims of narcissistic abuse; however, overall, I find that each of them shares so many of the same characteristics, they just might be displayed differently or not be evident at all to someone on the outside. That is not to say that those characteristics are not present. If anything, I think what is most accurate to say is that what causes them to be a narcissist, what is on the inside, is generally the same, however, it's the behavior or outward expression of what's on the inside that sets them apart.

For example, an overt narcissist is just as insecure as a covert narcissist, but the overt narcissist will mask their insecurity with charm and charisma, whereas a covert narcissist will hide it underneath a disagreeable and passive-aggressive exterior.

Grandiose or Overt Narcissist

Both **Grandiose** and **Overt** refer to the same type of narcissist. **Grandiose/Overt Narcissists** are out in the open, in-your-face, obvious, and have the stereotypical grandiose traits commonly thought of as narcissistic. These are the great white sharks of the narcissists. Their presence is large, loud, and lingering. They are typically the types of narcissists who are outgoing, larger than life, charismatic, and draw others into their orbit. They're the ones you want to be around and who make you feel privileged when they

want to be around you. They are often highly successful professionally or portray themselves as such. They'll be the most charming
person you can imagine as long as there is something that they
want from you. When faced with someone else's success, instead of
reacting with appreciation or admiration, a grandiose narcissist
will react with jealousy. They'll have in their mind that no one else
is impressive and will commonly compare themselves in a way that
positions themselves as better than others. The grandiose narcissist
projects an aura of self-confidence; however, the second they feel
threatened, their attitude will turn to one of ferocity.

Grandiose/overt narcissists want to feel special, important, and
admired. They want to be respected, revered, recognized as superior, and remembered. It may seem like a grandiose narcissist is
completely confident and has no fear, but ultimately, all of their behaviors are motivated by their greatest underlying fear—the fear of
not being good enough. The grandiose and abusive behaviors stem
from a need to avoid seeing and acknowledging their own flaws.

Vulnerable Narcissist

To say I have an issue with this term is putting it lightly. First of
all, in reality, every narcissist is vulnerable. That is one of the fundamental aspects of what causes pathological narcissism—a vulnerability to shame. It's just that the false confidence presented by a
grandiose/overt narcissist makes them appear as though they are not
vulnerable, whereas the quiet expression and victimizing tactics of
covert narcissists make them appear vulnerable.

Second of all, but most importantly, I believe that this label is absolutely detrimental to the cause of helping people avoid staying in
long-lasting narcissistically abusive relationships. As human beings,
we automatically develop compassion for those we think of as
vulnerable, which means we are more likely to provide grace and
not just second chances but third, fourth, fifth chances, and so on.
This is more likely to lead survivor-victims to stay in abusive relationships rather than leave because they feel bad leaving or saying
no to someone they perceive as vulnerable.

It is for these reasons that I prefer the term "covert narcissist" since they are supposed to encompass the same characteristics anyway.

Covert Narcissist

Covert narcissists are much less obvious. They tend to be more reserved and have traits such as avoidance, being melodramatic, and seeming miserable. They are typically more introverted, staying home and out of the spotlight, unlike overt narcissists. They are also more likely to victimize themselves in order to elicit sympathy. Their contempt for others will often be more obvious, even though this is a characteristic shared by other types of narcissists. Whereas an overt narcissist may be quite aggressive, a covert narcissist is more likely to be passive-aggressive, not that an overt narcissist won't ever be passive-aggressive.

Malignant Narcissist vs. Nonmalignant Narcissist

Malignant narcissists are the most severe and dangerous you can come across. Malignant narcissists are so far to the unhealthy end of the spectrum of pathological narcissism that they are sociopathic or even psychopathic. These are the types of narcissists who are devoid of empathy, not just deficient in empathy. Malignant narcissists can be described as malevolent, having a desire to do harm to another person. They are the ones who will make you feel bad because it makes them feel good and are the most likely to cause extreme forms of ongoing mental, spiritual, and physical injury to their partners. Both covert and overt narcissists can be malignant or nonmalignant.

How do malignant narcissists differ from nonmalignant narcissists? It often comes down to the

> **Growth Moment**
>
> If you have the companion guide to this book, the *Swimming with Sharks Growth Book*, take a moment here to check out the *What Species of Shark Are You Dealing With?* reflection page.

intent behind their behavior as well as the level of empathy they possess. Some narcissists truly don't understand the extent of the damage they cause. They're partly or mostly unaware of how their behavior hurts others and breaks down relationships. Nonmalignant narcissists don't consistently intend to hurt you even though that is typically the result of their behavior.

Chapter 20

THE NARCISSIST'S INNER WORLD

In this chapter, I will give you insight into what's really going on inside the narcissist, well, at least my theories. First, we'll explore the narcissist's fragile self-image through the analogy of an earthquake. Then, we'll discuss how to use your knowledge of their patterns to anticipate the strength of their reaction to a confrontation.

Narcissistic Earthquakes: Understanding the Narcissist's Fragile Self-Image

Think of how scared we are of being in a building when an earthquake strikes. How do we trust how well the building will stay standing? Imagine being in a building that has been specially constructed to withstand the strongest of earthquakes. If one hits, you might experience some mild anxiety, but you won't end up in a full-blown panic or running around the building screaming. You'll feel relatively secure and safe.

On the other hand, what if you lived in a home that your parents built with their bare hands years and years ago? Only, they weren't architects or carpenters. They just needed to quickly put a roof up over your head, so they fastened together what they could find, not taking the time to learn how to best construct a home and not paying enough attention to how they were building it or the materials they were using. When a board wouldn't fit where they wanted it to go, they would just yell and scream out of frustration while slamming their hammer down until it finally submitted itself into place. After the basic construction was done, they left it like that. They did not tend to flaws or cracks that showed up, because they either didn't know how to or didn't care enough to take the time to figure out how. All they cared about was that the structure at least stayed standing.

Now, imagine living in this old home as an adult. One day, you start to feel a rumbling sensation. You freeze, your heart beginning to pound a little. As you confirm that the rumbling isn't just in your head and that the floor beneath you is truly shaking, panic sets in. While it may not be a conscious thought, you know that when the foundation for this building was constructed, not much attention was paid to strengthening it or shoring it up to be able to withstand unsteady ground. At this point, the brain instinctually goes into survival mode in an effort to survive this threat to your safety.

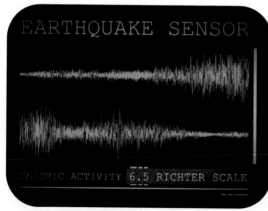

Every time someone challenges a narcissist, accuses them of something, or points out anything that makes them feel remotely vulnerable, it's as though the earth is quaking, leaving them acutely aware of their vulnerabilities and just how unsafe they truly are. Narcissists already feel so unsafe and vulnerable that admitting to their vulnerabilities feels like a threat, as though it will make the foundation crumble out from under the building.

Let's take the analogy a step further. Now, you're in a large apartment building that begins to shake. If there are other people in the building, as much as you may hope you would be the heroic type to sacrifice yourself in order to save everyone else, you are most likely going to do whatever it takes to save yourself. In your effort to save yourself, you push past others, possibly even knocking them to the ground and out of your way, because if they're in your way, they also pose a threat to your safety. Remember, this is your brain's most basic instinct kicking into overdrive, it's not something that would end up feeling like a conscious choice.

Now, imagine there's no way out of the building. There are no exit doors. The flights of stairs never arrive anywhere. You are simply unable to escape. The building never actually ends up collapsing though and the shaking eventually stops. With the current threat over, you return to your apartment and settle back into your routine. Unfortunately, you know that it's only a matter of time before another earthquake hits, and the cycle begins all over again. Living under this cloud of uncertainty and insecurity, you are never able to fully relax into a sense of calm and safety, because not only are you stuck in the poorly constructed building, you have no idea what it's like to live in a safe building.

If you've ever wondered what it's like in the mind of a narcissist, this is an apt analogy for their inner experience. They're never able to feel truly safe. Their lack of a secure foundation for their self-image leaves them feeling at risk at all times. The safe building I mentioned at the beginning of this section—that's how most of us feel within ourselves. If our world begins to shake a little because we're feeling emotionally threatened by someone else, it might feel a little scary, but we are able to regain our composure quickly because we have a strong emotional foundation.

Narcissists, on the other hand, live in a perpetual state of survival mode. A need to maintain an alert system makes them hypervigilant to threats. They've erected emotional walls in an effort to keep them safe, but this also keeps everyone else out, including you. It's made worse by their lack of personal insight. Not having an awareness of what is going on in their subconscious brain means that they don't know that it's something they can or need to change. And if you try to address it with them, you're perceived as a threat and immediately shut down. You never even had a chance to help them change.

Real World Example

One day, a child and her mother were going out to meet friends at a restaurant. Before going inside, the child let her mom know that something was sticking out of her nose. The child was shocked when her mom began to berate her. She thought she was doing something nice by letting her mom know before going inside. This mother, being the narcissist that she was, was so insecure that she couldn't emotionally accept that something as simple as her nose being unclean would happen to her, and she couldn't handle the discomfort it brought to her. So the mother's defenses went up, and she lashed out at her child, making it her daughter's fault that she felt uncomfortable within her own skin.

Threat Scale for Narcissist's Injury & Rage

Just as we use the Saffir-Simpson Hurricane Wind Scale to measure the strength of a hurricane in order to anticipate the level of damage it may cause when it reaches land, we can gauge the severity of a threat to a narcissist's self-image, how vulnerable it might make them feel, and how strong of a defense reaction they may have. This is useful to take into consideration as you begin to increasingly set boundaries with your narcissist. Anticipating the severity to which a narcissist will interpret any new boundary as a threat can help you prepare. By this, I mean that you can determine the extent to which you need to prepare emotionally (i.e. setting up your own emotional walls), or even physically (i.e. increasing physical distance, having a safe person nearby).

For example, you may determine that it is time for you to begin calling out your narcissist on their abusive language by telling them that you expect them to stop talking to you that way. You know them well enough to have a pretty good idea of what their reaction might entail. Considering this ahead of time, even if it's moments before you say something, allows you to prepare yourself to shut off your own emotional reactions to what they might say in return. This will help you to not become overwhelmed by your emotional codependency (the degree to which you feel responsible for the narcissist's emotions). If you think they might react with rage, be prepared to immediately exit the home and go for a walk or take a drive, returning only once you are sure they have calmed down, and it is safe to do so.

"You'll never be good enough."

—*The Subconscious Self-Talk of a Narcissist*

Chapter 21

NARCISSISTS AND SHAME

We are *not* born believing that we are *not* good enough. A toddler does not run around questioning how other people feel about them. If our childhood is for nothing else, it is to reinforce that we are inherently good enough. That our existence on this earth brings meaning and purpose to the world and to society. That we don't need others to make us feel good enough, because we simply are. That we can stand independently and confidently claim, "I am good enough just as I am." Unfortunately, it is our experiences with other people that chip away at this innate strength, such as the many moments when our parents yell at us, and we have no idea why, so we're left with the only explanation that makes sense—something must be wrong with us. Every time another child makes fun of us, a little more is chipped away. When a teacher scolds us in front of a classroom, we feel just a little less "good enough." There are so many factors in the world that dissolve our self-image.

It is the job of our parents or other caregivers to constantly reinforce the belief, "I am good enough." Although most often well-meaning in their efforts, far too many of them fall short of this responsibility. Falling short leads to the insecurities that nearly all of us wrestle with. But what creates a narcissist is far worse than just falling short. If we were able to rewind the movie that is a narcissist's life back to their childhood, we would most likely come across repeated moments when one or more of the adults in their life repeatedly contradicted the belief that they were good enough. These are what I call messages. Sometimes, the message is as obvious as a parent literally saying, "You'll never be good enough." Most of the time it's more subtle like, "What were you thinking?" or "I can't believe you would do that." It could even come out in the form of praising another child for being able to do something that their child couldn't. There are countless other examples of messages that teach a child that they aren't good enough.

The idea of not being good enough is the foundation of shame. I'd like to make a quick side note here that if you want to take a deep dive into understanding shame, I highly recommend checking out any of the work that Brené Brown has done. She refers to herself as a "shame researcher" and has spent many years not only researching shame, but writing about it in ways that have brought incredible healing and insight to thousands, if not millions, of people.

When it comes to shame and narcissism, it's extremely important to understand that shame is part of the foundation of pathological narcissism. A narcissist's pathological behaviors are rooted so deeply in shame that if shame were to not exist, neither would pathological narcissism.

Shame is also the reason why narcissists don't own up to their mistakes. To gain a better understanding of why this is, think of a house of cards. If you try to put anything heavier than another card on it, the cards collapse. The narcissist's distorted self-image is like a house of cards—it can't stand up to the extra weight of bearing responsibility for a mistake or admitting fault for having done something that could lead to them feeling shame.

*"Why did my mom
choose to hurt me like that?"
"Why does my husband
treat me this way?"*

Chapter 22

NARCISSISTS AND POWER

Inevitably, I'm asked questions like these. While it has become refined over the years, my answer now is, "Power." I explain that I don't mean power in the way we think of dictators seeking power. I'm referring to a simpler version of power, the type of power that allows someone to feel like they are in control, even though, deep down, they feel powerless in the world. I explain to my patients that the narcissist is not trying to hurt them for the sake of hurting them or from a desire to experience pleasure from their pain. That would make them a sociopath. The narcissist, rather, is seeking a sense of equilibrium and calm in the midst of a tumultuous storm raging inside of them. Their deep insecurity and desperation to avoid shame leads them to constantly feel unsafe. Feeling unsafe leads to further insecurity. As you can see, the cycle folds in on itself, and human instinct is to find a way to break such uncomfortable cycles. The narcissist's attempt to grasp onto some sort of power is out of an unconscious need to break the cycle. They are trying to gain a sense of power over their fear. Unfortunately, narcissists don't have the insight to understand that exerting power in that way is similar to taking a drug to numb or avoid emotional pain. The relief is momentary.

Brené Brown, in *Dare to Lead*, talks about power. She shares that Martin Luther King Jr. defined power as the ability to achieve purpose and effect change. As Brené aptly points out, this does not put power into a good or bad context. If we think of power from a neutral perspective, it helps us to see the narcissist's motivation from a neutral and objective perspective. Achieving purpose and effecting change can mean many different things to different people.

When I hear that definition, I can't help but associate it with a positive purpose and meaningful change. In writing this book, my purpose is to help others find a deeper understanding of narcissistic abuse, how it has impacted them, and how they can heal. I seek to make meaningful change in the world by reducing systemic narcissistic abuse through growth in knowledge.

However, if I take a moment to think about how Dr. King's definition of power applies to a narcissist in a neutral way, it is also very apt. Narcissists always have a purpose that they are trying to achieve, and they are constantly trying to effect change. For the narcissist though, that purpose is typically self-interested and an attempt to maintain positive feelings about theirself, thus limiting the amount of shame they experience. The change they are trying to effect is most likely that of manipulating another person into feeding their need for reassurance that they are good enough. So, when a narcissist is able to manipulate others into helping them avoid their own shame, they have gained a sense of power. The release of positive hormones that occurs when someone feels a surge of power only reinforces the behaviors that provided the power as ones to be repeated. Seeing this from a position of neutrality helps us to accept the narcissist's need for power for what it is, their own need to preserve their self-image. We don't need to see it as a good or bad thing. Neutrality helps us to become indifferent to it, which then helps us to feel less hurt. The less hurt we feel, the more we can accept them for who they are.

Chapter 23

NARCISSISTIC SUPPLY

I think of narcissistic supply as the emotional energy that other people provide to a narcissist, similarly to how food provides calories to our bodies which are then converted into energy. Because a narcissist is deeply insecure, they are unable to fully support their own emotional energy. This leaves them needing supplements. Whereas many of us only need a multivitamin to supplement our diet, a narcissist needs the equivalent of drinking three Ensure shakes a day in order to support their emotional energy needs.

Narcissists and
Their Drug of Choice

I can't help but associate the term "narcissistic supply" with "drug supply." To help better understand narcissistic supply, let's consider what keeps a substance abuser hooked to their drug of choice and evaluate how

narcissists experience others similarly. Much like someone using drugs to feel better by getting high, narcissists seek to feel better by experiencing a similar high. Only rather than substances supplying them with a high, they use other people to supply them with a high.

When we do something pleasurable or reach a goal, our brain releases dopamine, which stimulates the reward center of our brain, thus causing us to experience pleasure. If the narcissist is an extrovert, they already love being around people because of the natural high that comes from interpersonal interaction for them. Even if they aren't an extrovert, any narcissist is going to feel rewarded when anyone responds to them in a way that makes them feel better about theirself. You may be thinking, "Well, don't we all?" And you're right. The difference is that we can more easily experience pleasure from other things because we have a more secure self-image. Narcissists' low self-worth leads them to feel more dependent on external affirmation. And because this is the only way that they can feel better about themselves, the result is more rewarding to them. Greater reward equals greater dopamine release which equals greater pleasure.

So, when you respond positively to them or offer praise, their subconscious is like, "Oh yeah, this feels great! Let's keep this going." So they latch onto you and stick around as long as you are providing a steady supply of positive affirmations. Once you start holding them accountable or setting boundaries, and they no longer associate you with pleasure, they move on to someone else who will.

This helps explain the occurrence of narcissists moving from victim to victim. It also relates to my explanation of why you are not a magnet for narcissists (see later chapter). Furthermore, it helps to explain why you often end up feeling used within any relationship with a narcissist.

Narcissistic Supply Hopping: Moving from One Victim to the Next

A patient I worked with years ago shared that once they chose to no longer be a source of narcissistic supply to their partner, they noticed an interesting pattern within their narcissistic partner's moods and behavior. They could perceive when their partner was being unfaithful and when things were going well or not well within their extra-marital rela-

 Growth Moment

If you have the companion guide to this book, the *Swimming with Sharks Growth Book*, take a moment here to check out the *Narcissistic Supply* reflection page.

tionships based on the mood the narcissist displayed while home. When the partner was in a new relationship, they would act happier and more accommodating at home. It was also clear when the narcissist was getting tired of the other person because their mood became grumpy. This indicated the amount of narcissistic supply their partner was receiving from outside the home.

When it comes to explaining how this works, I like to use the analogy of an oil field. Under the earth's surface, there are pockets of oil. Sometimes people will drill down and find oil and sometimes they won't. When they do, they place a rig over the well and leave it to suck up the oil until the well runs dry. Once the well is dry, the rig is moved to another well where it can siphon off more oil supply, and so on. This is similar to a narcissist finding empathic people who provide narcissistic supply versus those whose emotional wells appear to be dry. If one person doesn't provide them with what they need, they will move on to someone else. Once they do find a full well, they will stay for as long as there is supply pumping up to them. If the supply stops, though, the narcissist will move on to someone else, regardless of the type of relationship or level of commitment they have made to the current source of supply.

Chapter 24

NARCISSISTIC PARENTS

My first experience helping someone who was suffering from narcissistic abuse at the hand of one of their parents, or in this case both, was during my sophomore or junior year of high school. One of my friends, we'll call her Coral, was deeply hurting. She was depressed and in a constant state of anxiety. It impacted her during and after school. Her relationships with others were damaged. In fact, looking back with the knowledge that I have now, I can see that her relationships with friends and boyfriends were developed based on dysfunctional patterns she had learned at home.

Coral struggled deeply with low self-worth because her parents were not only physically but also emotionally beating her down every day. They were so miserable within themselves that they felt compelled to drag their child down too. I did my best to help Coral cope with her situation and give her respite away from her home by regularly inviting her to mine. We prayed together regularly, and I gave her the space she needed to be able to process through all of her feelings. While we didn't know at the time that there was a specific name for it, I'm so glad that Coral was able to open up about her parents' narcissistic abuse. Had she not been open with me and a couple of other people about it, there is no telling how she might have coped with her trauma or what could have happened to her.

Being the victim of narcissistic abuse as a child has long-lasting and detrimental effects. Because many people don't realize that what they experienced was psychological abuse, they often find themselves in relationships as adults that mirror their relationship with their narcissistic parent. The abuse cycle continues for them and, unfortunately, often for their children as well.

While Coral and I lost touch in college, Facebook brought us back together from a distance. She got married and had her first child shortly after high school. They stayed together long enough to have a second child, but the marriage didn't last. I always wondered if her husband treated her like her parents did. Now, with two beautiful nearly-adult children, she is about to get married to her second husband. While it looks like she is living a happy life from the outside, I know that's what it looked like in high school too. I can only hope that she has found healing over the past twenty years and that she was able to break the cycle of abuse by being a healthy parent to her kids.

Love and Narcissistic Parents

We learn to love and accept ourselves from the love we receive as children. However, when we are raised by narcissists, every narcissistic trauma inflicted by a parent who shows any version of a lack of love (i.e. disappointment, scolding, shaming), blocks us from not only receiving love but from learning how to love ourselves. Every time the narcissistic parent says they're disappointed in us, every time we are scolded for making a mistake, every time we are shamed, we internalize that, while simultaneously being taught to be disappointed in ourselves, to scold ourselves for every mistake we make, and subsequently to shame ourselves.

Mothers & Daughters

If you feel like you've never been able to earn your mother's love or that her love is conditional, you are not alone. One of my patients shared that she spent years spinning her wheels trying to earn her mom's love and make her mom happy. It wasn't until she realized that it was her mom who was the unhealthy one, that she finally let her wheels stop spinning.

I've heard stories of narcissistic mothers who will future-fake their adult children. For example, one of my patients shared that her mother told her that when my patient had a baby, she would be present and by her side to help her take care of the baby. Once the baby came though, the mother showed up to meet her grand-child, but when the sleepless nights began, mom was nowhere to be found. And so, the disappointment continued.

Understanding Narcissistic Parents

Once you realize that one or both of your parents were, or still are (if they are still alive), narcissistic, you begin to go through a grief process. It's easy to fall into the trap of being angry in order to avoid the pain of feeling hurt or betrayed. And while these are valid emotions that you need to process, it becomes unhealthy when you stay stuck here. This is why it's helpful to begin to reframe your interpretation of your narcissistic parent(s).

Something that is important to keep in mind is that while your parent *was* being intentionally manipulative, they likely didn't have the insight to realize that this is what they were doing. I realize that this sounds somewhat paradoxical, but such is the nature of a nar-cissist after all. The narcissistic parent has a vague awareness that they are trying to get what they want, but because of their reduced empathy for your emotional experience, rarely do they have enough social awareness to realize that what they are doing is hurt-ful. This is really important for you to know because it's easy to jump to black-and-white conclusions about our narcissistic parent and vacillate between the angel and demon images of them. Doing this leaves us feeling confused and unresolved. You don't need to see them as one or the other though. You can acknowledge that there is both good and bad there at the same time. Changing to this perspective will ease the anxiety and hurt, bringing you understanding and peace.

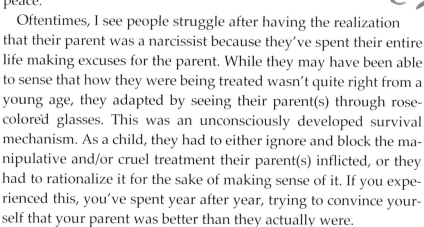

   Oftentimes, I see people struggle after having the realization that their parent was a narcissist because they've spent their entire life making excuses for the parent. While they may have been able to sense that how they were being treated wasn't quite right from a young age, they adapted by seeing their parent(s) through rose-colored glasses. This was an unconsciously developed survival mechanism. As a child, they had to either ignore and block the manipulative and/or cruel treatment their parent(s) inflicted, or they had to rationalize it for the sake of making sense of it. If you experienced this, you've spent year after year, trying to convince yourself that your parent was better than they actually were.

   No matter the circumstances that brought you to this moment, you have now been slapped in the face with the notion that your parent is not as "good" as you had convinced yourself they were. And for some reason, people have a tendency to instinctually swing the pendulum to the other side and start seeing their parent as a bad person. Perhaps this is to reconcile the new insight into the parent's unhealthy and hurtful behavior because it's tough to keep a parent in the framework of a good parent while also being aware of their mistakes. "If my parent were good, how could they have done those things to me?" we tend to ask ourselves. So the only way we know how to make sense of this is to turn them into a bad parent. This is our way of making meaning out of a story that doesn't make sense. Sometimes, the opposite is true. You may have spent your whole life thinking of your parent(s) as "bad" and not leaving any room for the good that existed there too.

The point I'm trying to make, though, is that you don't need to see them as one or the other, good or bad. They just are. Accepting them for who they are, without labeling them, is your key to moving forward and mending your soul. You need to let go of your inclination to judge them as good or bad and encourage yourself to be okay with seeing them in more simple and neutral terms—simply as they are. To bring this full circle, this is why I explain that it's important to know that most parents don't do these things with the knowledge that their behaviors are so hurtful. Knowing this makes it easier to accept them as they are, or were.

 Growth Moment

If you have the companion guide to this book, the *Swimming with Sharks Growth Book*, take a moment here to check out the *Narcissistic Parents* reflection page.

Chapter 25

OTHER NARCISSISTS IN OUR LIVES

Narcissistic relationships are not limited to those with parents or partners. They come in all shapes and sizes. You may have found yourself dealing with a narcissistic boss, coworker, friend, neighbor, church member, or even a pastor or other faith leader. In fact, now that your understanding of pathological narcissism has grown so much, there's a good chance that you will start realizing that multiple narcissists are already present in your life. Here are some examples of where you may encounter narcissists and how to deal with them.

Narcissists in the Workplace

I've been procrastinating writing this section because it feels a little too fresh and triggering. As a business owner, I employ quite a few people. Unfortunately, despite narcissistic abuse being my clinical area of expertise, a few narcissists have slipped through the hiring cracks. Each time this has happened, they cause significant distress over many months, and the energy and time that is wasted is a significant loss to not only the business but also my own well-being. The ups and downs are enough to cause motion sickness, and the uncertainty that accompanies this type of relationship is confusing and extremely frustrating. The pattern thus far has been that everything starts out great. At some point though, I start to notice some potential red flags. Due to the nature of narcissistic traits and tactics, it's rare that I can say with immediate certainty that what is happening is indeed stemming from narcissism. This leaves me in a holding pattern, hoping to be wrong, but watching and waiting for indicators that I'm not. I do my best to effectively utilize my leadership skills by compassionately addressing my concerns and lovingly guiding them toward healthy change. Inevitably, the employees' narcissistic behaviors escalate, and it becomes clear that long-lasting change won't happen.

As an employer, dealing with a narcissistic employee is beyond frustrating, so I can only imagine how difficult it is when you have a coworker or boss who is a narcissist. Just like every other relationship, regardless of any power differential, the key to surviving is setting boundaries, no matter how uncomfortable that might be. However, the way in which you set those boundaries with a workplace narcissist will be different from how you would with a partner or parent and depends greatly on their position relative to yours. If you are in a subordinate position, you won't necessarily want to declare that there will be consequences for boundary violations, because that could be perceived as a threat, which definitely won't go over well in the workplace. Your safest bet will usually be to gently establish boundaries as concerns arise.

For example, if your boss frequently asks you to stay late, rather than walking into their office one day and declaring that you no longer want to stay late, you might consider waiting to bring it up in response to a specific occasion on which they make the request. Let's say that the next time they ask, it happens to be the same night your kid has an important sporting event. You might respond, "As someone who values supporting our team, I would love to be able to help, but unfortunately, the timing that evening conflicts with an important engagement I already committed to. Can I help in some other way?" This is a much more effective way to maintain positive relations in the workplace than boldly establishing a blanket boundary that you will never stay late so you can be home for your kids. As true and valid as this might be, it's also a quick way to find yourself out of a job and replaced by someone who comes across as more of a team player. Having boundaries doesn't make you less of a team player; however, the manner in which you set them can greatly impact the perception of the degree to which you are one.

Another factor to consider when dealing with a narcissist at work relates to talking about them to others. It can be tempting to vent about your narcissistic boss, colleague, or subordinate while at work. When talking about the narcissist to others though, avoid using the term "narcissist," even with those you consider to be friends. You never know when or how it can come back to haunt you. Instead, opt for factual descriptors, such as the traits and tactics listed in chapter 6.

If you have a human resources department, you may be able to request a meeting to discuss your concerns and find out what sorts of options you have. Tread lightly and slowly here, gauging whether or not the HR rep will be on your side. Human resource departments are often geared to protect the company, not the employees. This may even be something you could clarify before opening up about your situation. Just as with other members of your workplace, when discussing the narcissist, be mindful of the need to be factual and limit opinion-based statements. As a therapist, it pains me to say this, but avoid language that will come across as emotional. While your emotions are valid, certain people are uncomfortable with emotions. And as wrong as it is, some of them will label you as a problem. Unfortunately, some people just like to make problems go away rather than resolve them. If you do feel the need to discuss your emotional responses to the situation, start slowly, observing how the other person responds, and adjust your disclosure accordingly.

While I want to empower you to stand up for yourself, I'm not naive to the fact that confronting pathological narcissism in the workplace, whether directly to the narcissist or to someone else, risks inflaming the situation and potentially the loss of employment. If you cannot afford to lose your job, before you start addressing your concerns at work, consider seeing a counselor for support and guidance. Check to see if your employer offers EAP services, which often provide a set number of free counseling sessions. You may find that talking about your situation with a qualified mental health professional provides you with all the tools you need to effectively handle your concerns in a nonconfrontational way, thus, maintaining the security of your job. With that being said though, if the way in which you are being treated violates any employment laws or causes you significant enough distress that it is interfering with your daily functioning, seek the assistance of a qualified legal, mental health, or other relevant professional immediately.

Narcissists in Places of Worship

Yes, narcissists can even be present in our places of worship, the places where we are meant to feel safe enough to be at our most vulnerable and literally bare our souls. Several terms have come up over the past few years to describe this occurrence. Church Hurt. Church Abuse. #ChurchToo. Much like most places and in most organizations, pathological narcissism can actually be quite rampant in churches. One of my patients was married to a pastor who was extremely narcissistically abusive to her and yet adored by his congregation. Another patient and her husband were professionally taken advantage of as staff members, and when they couldn't take it anymore and decided to leave, they experienced ridicule and became outcasts from those who were their closest friends within the church. That was until it started happening to them too, one by one.

Oftentimes, you'll see pathological narcissism present itself within the church as the need to maintain a pious image. Spouses of church leaders or prominent members will often betray their own values and beliefs, hide their opinions, and conform in ways that make them feel like they are losing their identities for the sake of keeping the peace, not just with their spouse but within the congregation as a whole. One incredibly baffling phenomenon is when narcissists within the church act as though the rules and moral codes don't apply to them. Well, I guess it's not completely baffling since they are narcissists, but it certainly stands out considering that, in general, moral codes of conduct are pretty well-set as opposed to outside of religious communities where there may exist some ambiguity or lack of consensus on what is morally acceptable or not, such as engaging in intimate relationships outside of marriage.

If you've ever wondered about or been fascinated by religious cults, those are often the manifestation of a narcissist's desire to "spiritually lead" others but not be perceived as hypocritical, so they create their own dogmatic belief system through a process of "renegotiating" Biblical meanings or principles in order to serve their own desires. Of course, that's just one example of many narcissistic reasons and manipulative ways in which cults are formed, but I'm sure there are plenty of books and documentaries that can better expand on that subject.

One of my own worst moments with a narcissist was at church. I had concerns about topics that the youth leader was introducing during Sunday school and youth group. The youth leader, in all the wisdom of his twenty-three years, decided to start bringing up topics like sex and pornography. My children, who at the time were thirteen and eleven, had no idea what porn was. So, of course, I was then stuck explaining it to them sooner than what I thought was an appropriate time/age. I didn't believe that my children needed to know that some adults choose to display their bodies and sexuality for everyone else to see. I felt there were other ways to establish a foundation for a healthy understanding of sex. And I definitely didn't want them to feel compelled to Google what it was.

My husband and I discussed our concerns with our friends, as it was their daughter who actually brought it to our attention. After a few other concerning situations happened, we approached our pastor about it. The details are a bit blurry now, but at some point, we were requested to join a meeting with our pastor, the youth leader, his wife, a fellow counselor, and I believe someone else I've blocked from my memory, for the purpose of directly addressing our concerns. Taking my notes with me, my husband and I sat down and began to share what had made us uncomfortable. We were calm and straightforward as we explained each point.

There was a moment after the dialogue began in which I felt compelled to turn to the youth leader's wife and let her know that we were not trying to address concerns with her, as we understood that she was not a member of the staff, even though she was by her husband's side whenever he performed his duties. It was at this moment that the tide shifted, although it actually felt like a tidal wave. The youth leader bolted up out of his chair in a huff and stormed out of the room then right back in again. He became so enraged that we were stunned and frozen. From that moment on he engaged in attack after attack, specifically toward me, or at least it felt that way. His accusations were baseless and irrational. Nonetheless, I felt compelled to respond and defend myself. The back-and-forth continued for at least forty-five minutes to an hour. The counselor who was supposed to be there as a mediator, or so I thought, did nothing to stop the attacks, and my pastor sat silently throughout as well. While I loved my pastor, and he is one of the sweetest men you could ever meet (definitely not a narcissist), the lack of support was a surprise to me. The meeting came to a close with a prayer, throughout which I sat sobbing uncontrollably. My husband and I left the meeting in shock over what had transpired. I was left feeling betrayed, gutted, and spiritually drained like I had never been before. I felt attacked on a psychological level as well as a spiritual level. In fact, as I'm sitting and writing about it right now, three years later, I feel shaky, and my heart is pounding.

The most ridiculous part of the whole thing was that once the meeting was over, they "announced" to us that the youth leader had found another job and was leaving our church. Each of the people present in the room allowed us to endure an hour and a half of berating and abuse for absolutely nothing. It was pointless to have had any conversation about our concerns when he was leaving anyway.

I had my suspicions of the youth leader being narcissistic already, but that meeting confirmed it and put the final nail in the coffin. In case you're wondering, my first major clue was a month prior when he and his wife were at the grand opening of my new group practice building. When I offered his wife a drink, she immediately looked to him for permission and allowed him to decline for her. That type of behavior is definitely a red flag. Add that to his condescending behavior of patting me on my head one day like I was a child or a dog, and I was definitely noticing a pattern.

> ❧ **Growth Moment**
>
> If you have the companion guide to this book, the *Swimming with Sharks Growth Book*, take a moment here to check out the *Other Narcissists* reflection page.

Part Five

NAVIGATING
FORWARD

Chapter 26

THE SEVEN STAGES OF SOUL-MENDING

Up until this point, you've likely been coping with your situation as a means to survive. But ultimately, we're all driven to do more than survive. We want to thrive! And right now, you're ready to get back to thriving, or perhaps thrive for the first time in your life.

Being the victim of narcissistic abuse can leave you feeling like holes have been ripped in your soul. Just as you mend a ripped pair of jeans, you have the power to mend your soul. Ultimately, this is the destination everyone longs to reach. The process of mending your soul will take time though. It may take months or often years, depending on the type and length of the relationships. That is okay. Have patience and grace for yourself as you go through this process.

From my years working with survivor-victims of narcissistic abuse, I have identified seven stages of *soul-mending*: Telling Your Story, Acknowledging the Abuse, Growing your Knowledge and Understanding, Retelling Your Story, Acceptance, Forgiveness, and Rebuilding Yourself. The reason why I use the term "stages" rather than "steps" is because following steps implies a specific order; however, the work you'll do to mend your soul will not be linear. Stages, on the other hand, allow you to pass through one and onto another in various orders. Some stages may need to be revisited at times in order to continue moving forward and some may be visited simultaneously. Ultimately, what I want you to know is that revisiting a stage does not mean that you are moving backward. No matter what you are going through, you are **always** moving forward because you can always learn and grow from the place you are currently in. Let's begin reviewing the stages.

Telling Your Story

🐚 Growth Moment
Take a moment here to crack open your journal and tell your story. Or, if you have the companion guide to this book, the *Swimming with Sharks Growth Book*, tell your story in the *Soul-Mending* growth activity.

When you set out on your journey toward soul-mending, you'll begin by telling your story. This may be to a therapist, a friend, a family member, or just yourself. Telling your story is like taking that first step toward something you want but are hesitant to go after because you're afraid of how painful it will be to get there. Once you do take that first step though, it gets easier to keep moving forward.

Acknowledging the Abuse

One path toward soul-mending requires acknowledgment of what has really been happening. This is a moment when you have to face the fact that you have been abused. If you cringed when I said that or just flat-out scoffed, you wouldn't be the only one. Most people I've worked with were very resistant to the idea of having been abused. We don't like to think of ourselves as being abused because in doing so, we think that we are making that part of our identity. Your identity though is what **you choose** for it to be.

> ❧ **Growth Moment**
>
> Take a moment to work through this on the *Soul-Mending: Acknowledging the Abuse* reflection page in the *Growth Book*.

You are not defined by what has happened to you or who has been a part of your life. While you remain resistant to acknowledging the abuse, you will not be able to truly feel like you have the power to mend your soul. If that's where you are though, that's okay. Try another stage to see how it might help.

Growing Your Knowledge and Understanding

Whether or not you're able to fully acknowledge that what you've suffered through is abuse, the Knowledge and Understanding stage is an important one. Growing in your knowledge of what narcissistic abuse is and why the narcissist chooses to behave that way enables you to make sense of something that is otherwise baffling. Like looking at a puzzle, it allows you to focus on the individual pieces and learn how and why all of those pieces fit together to make that particular picture. Knowledge provides clarity and understanding, each of which is an essential step toward acceptance.

> ❧ **Growth Moment**
>
> Take a moment to work through this on the *Soul-Mending: Growing Your Knowledge and Understanding* reflection page in the *Growth Book*.

Retelling Your Story

The more you retell your story, infusing it with the new knowledge and understanding you've gained, the more your level of acceptance will grow and the more in control you will feel. It's as though telling

> **🌰 Growth Moment**
> Crack open your journal again, or retell your story in the *Growth Book*.

the story repeatedly breaks the chains, one by one, that have imprisoned you within your pain. As you continue to gain more knowledge about narcissistic abuse and pathological narcissism, expect your story to evolve and bring you more clarity as well.

Acceptance

I want to make it clear that by using the term "acceptance," I do not mean that you are saying that what has happened to you is okay or that it is okay for the narcissist to continue to abuse you. **I am referring to the acceptance of the fact that you do not have the power to change the narcissist or the control you wish you had to get them to change.** Acceptance also does not imply that you remain in the relationship with the narcissist. Accepting the narcissist as they are and that you cannot change them will benefit you whether you feel obligated to maintain a relationship with them or decide to end the relationship.

In fact, accepting the narcissist as they are is the most powerful coping mechanism you can develop when you are stuck in a narcissistically abusive relationship. In doing so, you enable yourself to no longer be driven to change the narcissist into someone they are not, thereby freeing yourself of repeated disappointment. As a result, you will experience less friction and conflict with the narcissist because you will have accepted that you won't win the battle to change them.

Acceptance will bring you peace and make it easier to coexist alongside the narcissist. You will feel less triggered by their behaviors because you will no longer be expecting anything different. Acceptance is truly the key to releasing the power they once held over you. Except in moments of physical intimidation, control, or abuse, the reality is that the narcissist holds no power over you. It is your resistance to accepting them as they are which created the illusion of their power over you. This is an empowering realization. Knowing that you held the power all along means that you have the ability to release that illusion of power. It means that you are in control. If you get frustrated at yourself for not recognizing your level of control sooner, keep in mind that you didn't know better, so creating an illusion of power wasn't your fault. It was just you being human like the rest of us.

Acceptance is a process in and of itself, and one that isn't usually easy, so I've broken it down into four phases. Most people aren't ready to accept their situation at first, so the earliest phase is usually the "I'm not ready to accept ____" phase. After that, you enter the "I want to get to a place of acceptance ____" phase. The next phase is, "I am willing to accept ____." This phase is crucial because you can't truly accept something without being willing to accept it. The fourth and final phase of acceptance has been reached when you can say, "I have accepted ____."

> 💗 Growth Moment
>
> Take a moment to reflect on acceptance on the on the *Soul-Mending: Acceptance* reflection page in the *Growth Book*.

Forgiveness

From early childhood on, most of us are told that we need to forgive those who hurt us, especially if they are a family member or a close friend. This is certainly a popular topic in religious communities, particularly those of the Christian faith. And while they are well-meaning, it is often in these same communities that we are not only pressured to forgive others but made to feel guilty when we don't or can't. We're led to believe that something is wrong with us or that we don't have enough faith in God if we're struggling with forgiveness.

The truth is, though, forgiveness is an elusive concept for most of us. I think we're not really taught how to forgive because most people don't truly understand it themselves. We're told to forgive, but no one explains how forgiveness is accomplished. The fact that the concept is used as both a verb and a noun is confusing and rather misleading as well. Let me explain. When we use the term "forgive," we are referring to an action—something that we can do. However, when we refer to forgiveness, this is using it as a noun—something that we can possess or accomplish.

I make the argument that forgiveness is **not** an action that you do. Rather, I believe that forgiveness is a *state of being* that you *reach* as a result of *acceptance*. In my own life, while I used to attempt to *forgive*, experience taught me that it wasn't possible to implement the action of forgiving; rather, the act of accepting was what allowed me to get to a *place* of *forgiveness*.

Similarly, from my perspective, you can't just decide one day that you are going to forgive, and then *bam*, all is forgiven. In order to forgive someone or something, or reach a place of forgiveness, you first need to go through the process of acceptance. This is the part that most of us don't seem to know or understand because it's not talked about in this way.

Remember when you were a kid and wanted to ride a bike? You weren't able to just go outside, hop on a bike, and automatically be able to ride it. You had to first go through the process of *learning* how to ride the bike.

To give you another analogy, think of forgiveness as the fruit that blossoms from the branches of acceptance, which extend from the sturdy foundation of knowledge, the trunk of the tree. When it comes to fruit trees, you cannot just decide one day that you want to grow an apple. You have to first grow the apple tree. Similarly, we cannot just decide one day to forgive. Forgiveness only comes once we've accepted whatever it is that has hurt us which led to the need to forgive. And just like you don't have to think about how to make an apple tree sprout apples, you don't actually have to figure out how to forgive. It blossoms as a natural consequence of acceptance.

> You don't work on forgiving. You work on accepting, and then forgiveness comes as a result of acceptance.

Think of forgiveness as the destination at the end of your soul-mending journey. This isn't to say that your wounds won't be triggered in the future. But when they are, you'll already know the way back to forgiveness. No one reaches a place of forgiveness and stays there forever. The very nature of being human is that you will be repeatedly presented with the need to forgive.

*"Forgiveness isn't a journey,
it's the destination"*

How will you know you've reached a state of forgiveness? You will know that you've reached a state of forgiveness when you no longer feel the twinge of pain in your chest at the thought of whatever or whomever it was that hurt you. When you can think of or be in the presence of whatever caused you pain and simply feel neutral, you will know that you've achieved a state of forgiveness.

Forgiveness of Yourself

If you've been blaming yourself for what you've been through, you're not alone. It's not uncommon to assign fault to yourself rather than the abuser or to be angry at yourself for staying in the abusive relationship. Shame is often the root cause of this. With forgiveness of self though, comes a release of shame.

Many people consider it unimaginable to be able to forgive theirself. However, I want to reinforce that this is why we get stuck and unable to move forward. Putting pressure on ourselves to forgive (action), when it's not something we even understand how to do, creates a block we don't know how to get around. This is where it's imperative to circle back to acceptance. Accepting your anger is entirely possible. Accepting that you stayed is possible. And once this is achieved, forgiveness of yourself naturally follows.

Remember the context in which you chose to stay. Think about how you viewed the narcissist at that time—the hope you had for the future of the relationship—your optimism. Remember that you likely saw that person as strong and safe—of course you would want to be with someone like that. Because you started out the relationship thinking of the person as safe and secure, even once you realized they weren't safe, you continued to hold onto the idea, the fantasy, you had created because that's what you wanted to see. One part of your mind was in conflict with another. You may have been used to other people in your life leaving you, but this person didn't. At the time you saw that as love, not them seeking narcissistic supply.

"I ruined myself. I blame myself
so much for staying"
—*Anonymous patient*

Also, remember that blaming yourself and being angry at yourself makes you feel like you have control. Survivor-victims often do this so that when it comes time to consider finding a new relationship, it won't seem as scary because they think they have control. Just remember, though, while the only thing you have control over is your choices, the choice to blame and be angry at yourself isn't actually healthy, nor is it effective in preventing the hurt from happening again. You really are just ensuring a certain amount of hurt and misery in this moment and for however long you continue to blame yourself.

As you are working toward forgiveness of yourself, consider that sometimes your personality is a factor in why you chose to stay. Some people are driven to work at something to make it happen. In this case, you may have stayed in an effort to exhaust every option to make the relationship work. This way, you would avoid having any regrets. Even though it didn't work out in the end, you likely would have wondered if it could have, had you just stayed. Now, you can have peace that you exhausted all possibilities. As I hope you can see, trying to understand why you chose to stay and seeing it from that context makes it easier to *accept* the fact that you stayed.

Forgiveness of the Narcissist

The idea of forgiving someone who has hurt you so badly, maybe even been intentionally cruel to you and those you love, is a tough pill to swallow for many people. Many people are afraid that if they forgive the narcissist, it will make them vulnerable to allowing the narcissist back into their life. They use their lack of forgiveness almost like a shield against future pain. Some will say, "But they don't deserve forgiveness." Here's a different way of thinking about it. Forgiveness isn't a gift to someone else. It's a gift to yourself. Right now, whether or not the narcissist is still in your life, you are trapped in a prison of hurt, anger, disappointment, resentment, and all

> **Growth Moment**
> Process through the idea of forgiveness on the on the *Soul-Mending: Forgiveness* reflection page in the *Growth Book*.

the other emotions that result from NAb. Forgiveness, however, is the key that unlocks the door and releases you from that prison.

Rebuilding Yourself

We've discussed many of the devastating effects of being in a relationship with a narcissist: Shame, losing sight of who you are independent of the narcissist, lowered if not obliterated self-confidence, difficulty making decisions for yourself, a self-image based on what others think of you, uncertainty about what you want now or in the future, no longer believing in yourself, and the worst of all, loss of your self-worth.

If we consider **self-esteem** to be what we **think** and how we **feel** about ourselves, we can define **self-worth** as what we **believe** about ourselves, specifically, **believing whether or not we are innately worthy**.

Healthy self-worth is believing that:

You are worthy just as you are.
You are worthy simply because you exist.
You are worthy of acceptance.
You are worthy of compassion.
You are worthy of kindness.
You are worthy enough to experience joy.
You are worthy of love!

Because narcissists have such low self-worth, they project this perception onto you and tear you down bit by bit, block by block, until your view of yourself becomes completely dependent on how they choose to define you. This allows the narcissist to feel like they are in control, which abates their own anxiety over seeing what they subconsciously believe about themselves—that they are not good enough and therefore unworthy.

The truth is, **your worth exists whether you believe in it or not**. It's just that all of the abuse and manipulation caused you to develop a false perception of yourself as unworthy. Once you remember your true self-worth, you'll be able to rediscover, or discover for the first time, your voice, your power, your purpose, and your value. You'll be able to discover what excites you, what brings you joy, and what you're passionate about. This is how you rebuild yourself!

Rediscovering her voice was a powerful turning point for one of my patients during her process of soul-mending. She enthusiastically declared one session, "You can't muzzle me!" And even though she wasn't saying this directly to the narcissist, it didn't matter. All that mattered was that she believed it. That she believed in herself. That she believed she was worthy enough to have a voice. That she believed that she was worthy enough to **rebuild** herself.

> **Growth Moment**
> Explore how you can begin this last stage on the *Soul-Mending: Rebuilding Yourself* reflection page in the *Growth Book*.

Chapter 27

EMPOWERING KNOWLEDGE

The knowledge you have gained through this book so far has added to your understanding of the nature of narcissists as well as narcissistic abuse and how it has impacted you. Let's delve a little more into the things that I know will help in the process of mending your soul.

Knowing Why We're Drawn to Narcissists in the First Place

The Model Home

Have you visited a model home anytime recently? What appeals to you most about a model home? One of the things I love most about model homes is how clear of clutter they are. They present to me what my home has the potential to look like. While I can dream all day long of my house looking like a model home, and I certainly do my best to make it happen, the reality is that it never will. Living with two teenagers and a husband makes it impossible for my home to be clutter-free 100 percent of the time. Inevitably, my husband will leave his shoes lying around, which will give my daughter free rein to leave her art supplies scattered about, which may then lead my son to leave his dirty dishes on the counter. I could choose to hang onto the vision of my house maintaining a clutter-free status all of the time, driving myself crazy in the process by getting upset and everyone else frustrated by my constant fussing to clean things up. Or, I can accept that my home can be clutter-free part of the time and that the other part of the time when it is not is okay.

Similar to a model home, we're drawn to narcissists because of how they present themselves. They show us an illusion of what life could be and allow us to tap into a fantasy we have created of our perfect life. Narcissists make us think that we are getting a model home, when in reality, there is just as much clutter there as in any other house, they just don't allow us to see it. It is the fantasy that you fall in love with, because it's not possible to fall in love with what you can't see. The illusion of a person you were presented with is like a mirage. Even though it seemed real at the moment, it was never actually there. You only saw what you wanted to see and what the narcissist wanted you to see.

The Narcissistic Parent

I would estimate that about 80 percent or more of the time I have worked with someone who had a narcissistic partner, we ended up discovering that at least one of their parents was also highly narcissistic. Being drawn to someone who is similar to a narcissistic parent is an interesting phenomenon that occurs outside of our awareness. But why? Well, so far I've observed two possible explanations, comfort zones and narcissist stand-ins.

Comfort Zones

As humans, we like to stay within our comfort zones, even if those zones aren't healthy for us, because the familiar makes us feel safe. This relates to our fear of change which we discussed earlier in the book. The behavior patterns of our family of origin establish our interpersonal comfort zone. When the relationship between yourself and a partner includes dynamics that are similar to behavior patterns from childhood, you feel safe and comfortable, because it is similar to the environment in which you grew up. Oddly enough, if you were with a healthy partner, you likely wouldn't be very comfortable.

The Narcissist Stand-In

We are often drawn to potential partners who exhibit characteristics similar to those of the parent whose narcissistically abusive behavior deeply hurt us as a child. This person becomes our parent's Narcissist Stand-In. Even if it's difficult to recognize the narcissistic characteristics early on in a relationship, somehow our subconscious perceives them. The deepest part of our mind knows that we need to heal from our childhood wounds in order to live our fullest and healthiest adult life. *By drawing us to another pathological narcissist, our subconscious is hoping that the Narcissist Stand-In, despite their narcissistic traits, will choose to love us rather than abuse us, which is all that we ever wanted from our parent to begin with.*

As an adult, the experience of our parent's stand-in choosing to love us is intended to provide relief from the pain of our old wounds and subsequently allow us to heal. For this to work though, the Narcissist Stand-In would have to miraculously change from someone who is narcissistically abusive to someone who is empathic and caring. As we established in the Shark Tale Paradigm, this scenario is unrealistic and won't occur if the stand-in is a pathological narcissist as well. So what you end up finding yourself in is a Narcissist Loop, a cycle of staying with a narcissist based on an unrealistic hope that they will change or a cycle of moving from narcissist to narcissist out of a subconscious effort to heal your childhood wounds.

While choosing to stay in your comfort zone or finding a narcissist stand-in happens outside of your awareness, having gained that awareness now will help you to figure out when you're being drawn to someone just because they are similar to your narcissistic parent.

Knowing That You Are NOT a Narcissist Magnet!

Nearly every woman I've worked with has expressed a concern that they will end up in the same cycle of abuse with the next man. Each of them creates a narrative that includes the idea that they inherently attract narcissists, like sharks attracted to blood. Only they typically refer to being a magnet, not chum.

If you're recovering from a narcissistically abusive relationship, it's reassuring to know that you aren't projecting an invisible magnetic force that draws every pathological narcissist within a ten-

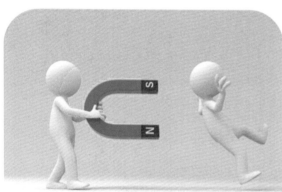

mile radius to you. Rather, when you come across one by happenstance, your empathic, loving, and giving nature provides an easy source of narcissistic supply, so they tend to latch on.

Did you ever play that game with a Velcro-covered disc that you put over your hand and throw a tennis ball back and forth with someone else? The concept is that the tennis ball sticks to the Velcro making it easy to catch. In this analogy, the narcissist is the tennis ball. Everyone else in the world is either a disc covered in Velcro or a disc with no Velcro. A disc with Velcro is a highly empathic person. Narcissists just sort of go around throwing theirselves at all the discs in the world, and when they hit one with Velcro, they stick and stay. There's no rhyme or reason to it. There is no magic quality in the Velcro that makes all tennis balls attracted to it. It's just happenstance that they found you, but once they did, you gave them exactly what they wanted so they stayed.

Knowing That You Are Grieving

Loss is a powerful force in our lives. As humans, we dread the pain that comes with loss and do everything we can to avoid it. There are many losses that come from a relationship with a narcissist. The realization that the person you love is a narcissist means that you have lost who you thought they were. Accepting that they will not change is a loss of the fairy tale, the fantasy you believed would come true. You are grieving the loss of what you thought your relationship could be. If the relationship has ended, you are grieving its death. You are grieving the loss of the future you had envisioned. You are grieving the loss of the life you had and the life you pictured yourself having. Sometimes it means grieving the loss of wealth and financial independence. Some are grieving that their children or grandchildren will not have the type of parent or grandparent you thought they would have. Many grieve the loss of time with their children, because they are forced to share custody. Most grieve the loss of the time that they feel was wasted on the narcissist.

We all dream of what our family might look like, what holidays will be like, what vacations will be like, or what we'll do once we reach retirement. These are all dreams that are lost when you figure out that you've built them on the premise that the person you love will always be there for you in the ways that you need, in the ways that they made you think they would be and yet they aren't.

Just the act of naming the feelings you are having as grief is empowering. Recognizing that they are healthy emotions as well as a normal part of this process allows you to accept your grief and experience it. Without this experience, you won't be able to pass through it and move beyond it. So allow yourself to grieve!

Knowing How to Regain a Sense of Control

Feeling like you aren't in control of your own life is common when dealing with a narcissist. What I find most helpful is to understand that **the only thing we can control in life is our choices**. Nothing else. We do not have control over any of the people in our lives. We don't even have control over the functioning of our own bodies. What we do have control over is our choice to put healthy food into our body to help our body function better. We have control over our choices in how we treat others, which impacts their behavior. Sometimes we allow ourselves to think that this is control, but it really isn't.

Operating under the illusion that we have the ability to attain control but never actually gaining it is a contributing factor to anxiety. The best way to reduce anxiety and regain a sense of control is to accept that, other than your own choices, you have no control.

The best way to reduce anxiety and regain a sense of control is to accept that, other than your own choices, you have no control.

"How do I know I won't end up in another narcissistic relationship?"

Chapter 28

JUMPING BACK IN

In *Shark Beach*, a documentary in which Chris Hemsworth investigates how we can live more harmoniously with sharks, Mick Fanning, a three-time surfing world champion shares the story of his encounter with a shark during a surf contest. He describes hearing a splash behind him, just before the shark bumped into him and subsequently smacked him in the face with its tail. Today, the surfer explains that even though he doesn't hesitate to get back in the water to continue surfing, he is much more mindful of his surroundings and watches the water around him more carefully. He also shares that he is easily startled by splashing noises behind him.

Much like the post-traumatic stress that Mick experiences, you may experience the narcissistic abuse stress symptoms we discussed earlier in the book. That doesn't mean that you can't begin to dip your toe back in the water. Soul-mending will be an ongoing process, and it's okay if you experience some discomfort in the meantime. Let's talk about how you can overcome the fear that underlies that discomfort.

Overcoming Your Fear

It's very normal to be afraid that you will end up in another narcissistic relationship. You've been deeply hurt, you've struggled to feel in control, and it was difficult breaking free. Now that you finally have taken back control over your life, it's natural to fear losing it once again. Here's the thing though—you do not need to be afraid. Fear gets you nowhere. Literally NOWHERE! In fact, for many of you, fear is most likely what kept you in a toxic relationship, to begin with. Furthermore, there is no such thing as a healthy dose of fear in any situation other than one that is life-threatening. To ensure that you end up in a situation that makes you happy and brings you joy, all you need is LOVE! I'm being serious here. Love is the only guide and roadmap you could ever need. Think about it, when was the last time that fear got you where you wanted? Consider the last time you had to make a decision. How might it have impacted your decision-making process if you had asked yourself, "Which choice comes from fear and which choice comes from love?" Would it have made it faster, less complicated, or allowed you to feel more confident in your decision? It seems too easy and too good to be true, but I promise you, this works. And not only does it work when it comes to fear of ending up in another narcissistic relationship, it works in literally every situation you can imagine.

Here's a great example for the parents out there. How many times have you gotten upset at your kids for having a messy room? Let me ask you something. Where do you think that frustration comes from? If you said that it's because you love your kids, and you want them to grow up knowing how to take care of themselves, or some version of that, just imagine me pressing a big red button right now that makes that awful "eeeehrr" sound indicating a wrong answer. I guarantee you that your concern over your kid's messy room is 100 percent connected to your fear of failing as a parent. Whether you are afraid that other people will see their room and judge it, your kid, or you for allowing it to be so messy, or it's that you are afraid your kid will grow up to be an adult who has no idea how to keep a clean room, it always traces back to a fear of being judged and fear of having failed at parenting. Here's the reality though. What you are doing by getting mad and fussing at your kid about their messy room is creating an insecurity within them by fostering their own unhealthy fear. And the most important point to make here is that as long as you show your kids you love them, and they feel unconditionally loved, you literally cannot fail at parenting. Unconditionally loving your children is the only way that they will learn to unconditionally love themselves. Also, as a side note, most kids will grow up and find value in keeping things tidy once they have their own space over which they feel a sense of ownership. And for those who don't, sometimes that's a sign of genius! So next time you're tempted to fuss at your kid about their messy room, pause and ask yourself what the loving way to handle it is. Encourage them to keep their space clean without shaming them for not. Let them know that picking up after themselves is not only loving toward you, it's also loving toward themselves to live in a clean environment.

So, how do you apply this concept in a way that will protect you from future toxic relationships? Let love be your guide in the same way. The moment you question someone's intentions, even if it's the first time meeting them, consider what the loving thing would be to do for yourself and cautiously evaluate if any other red flags appear. If you begin to doubt whether or not to stay in a relationship, ask yourself if you would be staying out of love or fear. Ask if the choice that would be most loving to yourself would be checking out of the relationship. Keep in mind that loving someone else does not mean that you sacrifice how you are treated. So if you're making sacrifices, rather than compromises, it's time to reevaluate. This applies to any relationship, not just romantic ones. Make sure that

> **💗 Growth Moment**
> Explore your fears on the *Jumping Back In* reflection pages in the *Growth Book*.

there is a healthy balance between loving yourself and loving the other person. When it feels skewed in the direction of the other person, consider why that might be.

Assessing for Red Flags Early in a Relationship

The number one requested resource by all survivors of narcissistic abuse is most certainly a list of red flags that someone might be a narcissist. It has taken a long time, but I've accumulated an extensive list of red flags, based on surveying numerous victims of narcissistic abuse to find out what, in hindsight, they see as things that were red flags at the beginning of their relationship but were not aware of at the time.

The Shark Detector includes numerous options of what you can address or directly ask about when you are dating someone new. I do want to caveat this by saying that most of these ideas come from anecdotal stories shared in therapy, my own relationships, and those of family members, as well as observation of others. These are not conclusions made from formal research studies. Also, because these are mostly from the anecdotal stories I've heard from women describing their male partners, I am going to choose to stick with the corresponding pronouns most of the time.

Many of the suggestions in the Shark Detector require you to actively "fish" to see if there's a bite that suggests you potentially caught a shark. This may be completely within your wheelhouse or it might make you uncomfortable. I want you to know that there is nothing wrong with taking an active stance, rather than a passive, wait-and-see approach. Dating is much like interviewing someone for a job—just with a lot more physical contact than you would hopefully experience during a job interview. You wouldn't interview an applicant without asking probing and specific questions, then hire them with the idea that if they don't seem qualified then down the road you'll just fire them. There is no shame in entering dating with the same idea in mind—just don't make it sound like an interview!

> ❦ Growth Moment
>
> Take a moment here to list out the red flags you saw at the beginning of your relationship on the *Jumping Back In: Flags* reflection page in the *Growth Book*.

SHARK
DETECTOR

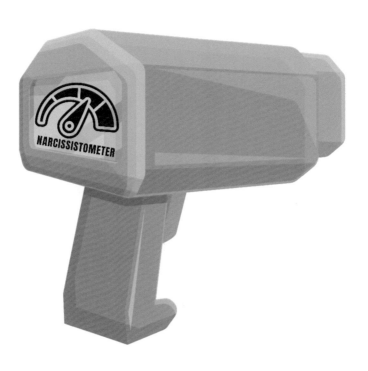

SHARK DETECTOR

The Shark Detector can be used to reflect on the behavior of anyone in your life, whether they are someone you are dating or a random person you encounter at a soccer game. I'm sure you could fill up an entire book with examples of red flags, but those I'm sharing here are ones that I've kept track of in my clinical work and personal life. Some of them may not make sense unless you've faced the same thing. But that's a good reflection of what a relationship with a narcissist can be like—the things they do or say leave you scratching your head and saying, "Huh?" because they're completely illogical or irrational. This list will at least give you some common themes to look out for. Some may not be relatable if you haven't experienced them while others may resonate greatly.

As you review the examples below, keep in mind that displaying a couple of these red flags does not make someone a narcissist. What *does* indicate that someone is a potential narcissist is noticing a *pattern* of numerous red flags, typically over a period of time. If you only notice one or two early on, keep an eye out in case others pop up. They don't usually all come out right away, and they don't have to show up around the same time to indicate a pattern.

 **Growth Moment**

Access the expanded version of the *Shark Detector* in the *Growth Book*.

First Date Dynamics

▦ What is the flow of the conversation?

- ☐ Either making conversation all about theirself or all about you.

- ☐ Talk constantly without leaving space for you to contribute to the conversation.

- ☐ Don't ask about you, in a deep way, or at all.

▦ Are they really listening to you?

- ☐ Not responding to your emotional expression.

- ☐ Quickly saying okay, gotcha, almost as though cutting off and impatient to move on in the conversation.

- ☐ Pay attention to the nonverbals of someone who is clearly uninterested.

▦ Do they name-drop?

- ☐ We all try to impress a person we're on a first date with. The question is, what are we using, doing, or saying to impress the other person?

- ☐ Try to impress you with who they are or who they've been, or who they've known or met.

- ☐ Try to impress you with external factors, other than theirselves, not about quality time with self and family.

- ☐ Kids go to preppy private schools based on school name recognition.

☐ They are all about the names of schools, colleges, universities, corporations, or other organizations.

Whom are they trying to impress?

☐ Do they act flirty with the waitress or anyone else?

Do they accuse you of anything?

☐ I've heard of one partner accusing the other on their first date of looking at the waiter like they wanted to sleep with them (however in much more vulgar terms).

Do they act one way with you and another way with other people, or the same way with everyone?

☐ Are they nice to you and mean to others, or vice versa?

☐ Makes you feel like you're special, but then acts similarly to other people in front of you, making you question if you are special to them.

Is their behavior condescending?

☐ Patting the top of the head of another adult.

☐ Speaking to you or someone else as though they are dumb.

☐ Referring to a woman, "She's wife material."

Do they seem to have an uncontrollable or awkward need to share what they need/want out of a relationship?

Are they overly doting on you?

Do they repeatedly ignore you?

Entitlement

 Expecting to be treated a certain way based on who they are.

Belonging to exclusive clubs and organizations.

This Isn't Broadway

Does it seem like everything is a show?

- ☐ Narcissists flaunt who they are and what they've done to make themselves stand out.
- ☐ Really big into their alma maters.
- ☐ Snazzy dressing to get attention.
- ☐ Has lots of parties.
- ☐ A LOT of "friends."
- ☐ Treats everyone like they are family members and can talk to them like they do their actual family members (in a way that's just too much—may seem sincere, but your intuition tells you that something feels off. Or they act the same with everyone, which makes their attitude toward you feel less sincere.)

Past Conflict & Admitting to Flaws/Faults or Laughing at Theirself

☐ Ask how they have resolved previous disputes (don't just look for communication skills, look for someone who admits flaws—this is healthy).

  ☐ A narcissist won't admit that they're wrong.

  ☐ They won't talk about their flaws, failures, or vulnerabilities.

  ☐ They won't express what their own mistakes were in their past relationships—will blame the exes.

☐ Pay attention to whom they blame.

  ☐ If they talk about issues at work, are they always blaming someone else?

  ☐ Can they take responsibility for their own mistakes?

☐ Can they laugh at theirself?

  ☐ Narcissists typically don't laugh at theirselves and get highly offended and often aggressive when someone teases or pokes fun at them.

  ☐ Isn't into sarcasm or is uncomfortable with sarcastic jokes that others might make. May be able to dish it out but can't take it.

Trashing Exes

- Ask about their previous relationships.

  - ☐ Talks about exes being super crazy, ridiculing their previous victim—making them seem unreasonable.

  - ☐ Says the ex was too clingy or needy or didn't give them their own space. If they don't see that as being wanted, then that's an issue.

  - ☐ Phone rings while on a date early on in a relationship, you hear someone yelling on the phone. Your date says, "Oh, I don't talk to them. They're crazy."

    - ☐ If you get up and walk out on that date, explaining that you don't get involved with things like that, does the person say to you, "Oh, no one's ever challenged me like that."

  - ☐ They say to you, "I never thought my partner would be strong enough to leave me."

  - ☐ Do they say that all of their exes were broken or damaged?

Content of Conversations

 Is there a negative or positive theme in their conversations?

- ☐ Gossiping about others.

- ☐ Critical of others.

- ☐ Joking of specific groups of people related to firm prejudices and expressing a sense of their own superiority (i.e. racist, sexist, or LGBTQIA+-phobic jokes, among others).

- ☐ Complains a lot.

- ☐ Complaining over and over about the amount of work and amount of time spent on something, but they don't do anything to change it and are resistant to any suggestions for change.

Vulnerability

This is going to be your greatest litmus test, not only for gauging how likely someone is to be a narcissist, but also for how ready someone is for a healthy relationship. Because narcissists have such a fragile self-image, being vulnerable is dangerous. It threatens their stability, because vulnerability creates a fear of cracking their foundation and crumbling down. Picture a building after a strong earthquake.

Your Interpersonal Dynamics / Response to Your Attention

▣ If you find yourself acting "clingy," pay attention to how they react.

☐ If the person tells you that you are too clingy or needy, leave right away. First of all, think about how they'll be with a child, because they are really clingy and needy. And second of all, most healthy people want to spend time with the person they're dating and feel wanted and needed. If they are rejecting your presence or calling you needy, that means that they aren't meeting your needs.

▣ Pay attention to their attitude surrounding trust.

☐ Do they expect you to trust them implicitly? Do they make you feel guilty if you question something?

▣ "God has been speaking to me."

▣ Telling you that you can talk about anything with them and then reacting poorly to what you say or using it against you.

▣ Telling you that "you aren't over your ex."

▣ "It's not my fault you feel that way."

▣ "I'm sorry you feel that way."

Overly Romantic
(Love Bombing)

 Try saying no!

- ☐ Pursuing strongly, even when you say no.
    - ☐ Real-life example: Saying no to someone because they used to date your sister, but they continue pursuing you in a very pushy way. Sometimes they will react angrily.
- ☐ They get mad because you cancel or change plans or ask them to leave because you need to do something else.
- ☐ They use the shotgun effect. Use every trick in the book until one sticks. All five love languages. Flowers, compliments, quality time, etc.

Family of Origin

Ask about their relationship with their mother/father.

- ☐ An intense relationship with mother—unhealthily strong attachment. Their mother comes before you.
- ☐ Avoids taking you home to meet the family. Or, it could be that they introduce you too quickly.

Friends

 Are you on display or hidden?

- ☐ Hiding relationship status (or hiding it from some people but not others) such as on social media.
- ☐ Sharing something about your relationship (timing of it) in front of friends, and they make an odd face that doesn't make sense at the time.
- ☐ They'll only come to your place and not invite you to theirs.

 Pay attention to how they are around their friends.

- ☐ Showing you off to friends or others right away, and something feels off about it. You might feel like you're being put on display, rather than getting to know friends. Not interested in your opinion of their friends.
- ☐ If their relationships with their friends seem superficial vs. deep. Meet the guys at the club vs. here are my childhood friends who know and love me.
- ☐ Sometimes, they won't even introduce you to their friends. This could be because they don't have any (red flag) or it could be because they don't want you to meet them for some reason (red flag).

- ☐ Are they social friends, are they work friends (which could say more about them being narcissistic or could be the opposite)—depends on what the introduction is like.

- ☐ Did they talk you up as they introduced you, or did they allow you to talk about yourself?

    - ☐ If they're worried about you making them look bad, they would control the conversation and introduction.

- ☐ Do they stay with you at a party?

- ☐ Do they have their "own friends" that they keep separate and don't integrate with you?

⊞ How do they define friendship?

- ☐ A LOT of "friends."

- ☐ Gossiping about others.

⊞ How do your friends react to them?

- ☐ Everyone else said that they were an a**hole and didn't understand why you were with them.

⊞ How do they treat other people?

- ☐ If they're mean or narcissistically abusive to others, then they can and likely will be that way to you.

Their Personal Identity

 How do they seem to define themselves?

- ☐ By their relationship with others (i.e. Knowing someone else with power or prestige).
- ☐ By their career.
- ☐ By their partner's career (i.e. Behaving as though they are special because they are a military spouse).

 Juniors—naming a child after theirself.

 Overly concerned about their looks—everything needs to be perfectly coiffed.

Careers

 Ask about their job/career.

- ☐ Successful people operate in a world that is rigged for narcissists—so they're often more financially capable of providing.
- ☐ Not doing a job because they love it, because it's their passion or calling. Doing it only because it brings them success and money.
- ☐ If they are in a job and can say that they are successful but

not happy—could indicate that they just don't know how to perceive their dreams or have been taught that their dreams are stupid or that they should only pursue a career for "security" to be safe, rather than pursuing for happiness.

- ☐ Jobs that offer power or prestige (doctor, lawyer, law enforcement, military, politicians—jobs that have people's lives or well-being in their hands).
- ☐ Not always a narcissist if they enjoy talking about the benefits of their job and how they help people.
- ☐ Seems like they're never satisfied with their job, because it doesn't make them special.

⊞ Narcissists often name their businesses after themselves.

⊞ Believing they are indispensable to their job. "They couldn't do this without me."

⊞ Fires or sabotages others for the sake of maintaining control and/or superiority within their company.

Catch and Release

If you notice a strong pattern of narcissistic behaviors, don't be afraid to end the relationship. The earlier it is in the relationship, the easier it is to release them. If you're afraid of making a mistake, talk to others, including a therapist, about your concerns and the patterns you've been noticing. Ask friends and family to give you an honest opinion of what they think of the person. Of course, take into consideration the motivation behind their assessment. For example,

I've known people who were strongly encouraged to stay in unhealthy relationships by their mothers or fathers because the person they were dating was "successful" or "had a good job." Typically, you'll get the most honest assessment if you ask someone who does not have a vested interest in you remaining in or getting out of a relationship.

EPILOGUE

Parting Thoughts on the Shark Tale Paradigm

Think of all the people who feel stuck in narcissistically abusive relationships. If awareness of the true nature of narcissists were as common knowledge as the nature of sharks is, including their unwillingness to make long-lasting change, imagine how many people would rescue themselves from toxic relationships early on. Envision countless lives being saved from the pain of narcissistic abuse. Picture children being raised in healthy households rather than dysfunctional ones because their parent chose a healthy partner rather than a toxic one. The ripple effect of adopting the Shark Tale Paradigm on a societal level could have an unimaginable impact on the health of individuals, families, and society as a whole. At the very least, I hope it has a positive impact on you.

Before we literally close the book on this, I'd like to leave you with one more story—but two tales—fairy and shark.

The Tales of Elizabeth and the Doctor

The Fairy Tale

Elizabeth, a mild-mannered young woman, spent her days working at the local medical school as an administrative assistant. She was satisfied within her job. Serving others suited her well. Sensitive and empathic, she felt a sense of purpose in pleasing those in her life. She'd been like this since a young child when her mother disengaged from her to focus on her own personal interests. Unknowingly, Elizabeth became a pleaser because that was the only time she received positive attention from her mother. Her father was around, but he kept his physical and emotional distance, a coping mechanism to keep the peace with his wife. In Elizabeth's youngest years, it seemed that no matter how he interacted with his sweet girl, it was always wrong, finding himself constantly scolded by his wife for how he played with Elizabeth, how he talked to her, how he handled her misbehavior, how he fed her, and so on. Neither Elizabeth's mother nor father had any idea how their choices were shaping their daughter into the vulnerable prey she would become as an adult.

Each fall, the medical school ushered in a new batch of eager students, ready to take on the world. Elizabeth had worked there for a few years, well acquainted with the staff and students. This particular fall though, she caught the attention of one of the new students. He was tall and mildly handsome, but what he lacked in attractiveness, he made up for in charm. Charisma oozed from his pores. He was intelligent and clever, and whenever he spoke, everyone seemed to listen.

Elizabeth was eating her lunch on a bench outside under one of the many trees on campus when Mark walked by. He stopped, his own lunch in hand, asked if he could sit with her, and introduced himself. Elizabeth assumed he had mistaken her for another medical student and quickly tried to clear up the confusion. However, Mark was quick to point out that he knew exactly who she was and that he had noticed her in the nearby building shortly after orientation. Elizabeth was flattered. The rest of their lunchtime flew by, the conversation flowing smoothly and without the slightest hint of awkwardness. When they finished their sandwiches, Mark walked Elizabeth back to her desk and asked if he could see her again that evening. Elizabeth, without any hesitation, agreed and told Mark when she would be done for the day. He promised to meet her back at her desk at that time.

Four hours later, Elizabeth packed up her belongings, excited for what the evening promised. Five minutes later, no Mark. She found some extra work and kept herself busy for the next thirty minutes, just in case one of his classes ran late. When there was still no Mark, she decided to leave and go home, disappointed and sad. She ate alone in her apartment that evening, scolding herself for being so stupid as to think that such a charming guy, a medical student with so much potential, would have any interest in her.

Embarrassed, Elizabeth dashed to her desk the next morning, praying that she wouldn't cross Mark's path on her way. She didn't see him all day, relieved but also disappointed. Even though she had been hurt that Mark didn't show up for her the night before, she couldn't stop him from consuming her thoughts all day. As the work day ended, she packed up her belongings once again, this time conceding to the inevitable solo dinner for yet another evening. Stepping around her desk, a thick voice startled her, "I thought you might need one of these." With instant recognition of the sound, a smile crept to her face, and she looked up. Mark was there, umbrella in hand, ready to escort her to her car. Elizabeth hadn't even realized that it had started pouring rain outside. Trying to tell herself that she was only relieved to have been provided shelter from the downpour, she knew that was a lie. If Mark had shown up empty-handed, she would have been happy to be drenched walking alongside him. It didn't hurt though, to feel like he had come to her rescue with something as simple as an umbrella.

As they walked through the rain, he made his excuses for standing her up the night before, explaining that he had been in the middle of a study group and lost track of time. While it didn't feel quite right, Elizabeth accepted the excuse as a valid explanation and told herself that doing well in medical school was far more important than going on a date with her. Little did she know that rationalizing Mark's empathic failures would be her go-to thought process for the next ten years.

Elizabeth and Mark were married for three years when she questioned him about a troubling discovery. "Who are you sending these text messages to?" Her voice quivering with fear and anger, Elizabeth did her best to confront him as calmly as possible.

Mark didn't waste any time launching into an angry tirade with fists clenched. "You of all people shouldn't be questioning me about being unfaithful! Everyone knows you can't be trusted!"

In reality, Elizabeth was faithful. Mark clearly wasn't. But that didn't seem to matter. If Elizabeth were honest, this was a recurring theme throughout their relationship. Mark operated like he was superior to her in every way. That played out in various ways, including anger outbursts (rage), emotional unavailability, bullying, putdowns, and not validating her thoughts or feelings.

Like any person in a relationship, Elizabeth had her faults. No one would have characterized her as a "nitpicker" though. Still, whenever she questioned Mark about something like significant financial transactions that didn't add up, she got blamed instead. He accused her of being financially irresponsible, a poor housekeeper, or spending too much time with friends, among other accusations depending on the scenario. The tables always got turned on her.

What was the result of the infidelity confrontation? Elizabeth was labeled as the guilty one by Mark. Deep down, she knew she wasn't in the wrong in this matter. But her emotions betrayed her. She was blamed as the problem so often when she wasn't that she started to believe it. She now felt false guilt that seemed impossible to shake.

Elizabeth eventually stopped questioning Mark whenever huge inconsistencies surfaced. She'd only feel worse about herself, which was the last thing she needed. Already the daily anxiety and guilt she now lived with were suffocating.

Why does my anxiety always get worse? she wondered. Before marriage, she considered herself brave, energetic, happy, and mostly worry-free. But Elizabeth was now in a state of perpetual "self-confidence bankruptcy."

When she discovered the dreaded text messages, much of her anger and fear were even more significant than the landmark betrayal of adultery. Elizabeth knew she wouldn't be able to work things out as a "normal" couple would. At least that might have brought some consolation, however small. Worse yet, she'd feel like the perpetrator, when she was the real victim of unfaithfulness.

Elizabeth asks herself, *How did I get here? What did I ever see in him?*

Elizabeth's life felt like a giant void, with each day growing worse than the one before. She initially hoped to learn more about herself through her relationship with Mark as healthy relationships should allow. But her reality was the exact opposite. Each day hurdled her headlong into feeling less sure of herself. And she gave up more hope of ever finding her more focused purpose in life.

She felt trapped in a relationship and life she wouldn't have wished on her worst enemy. Elizabeth desperately wanted to walk out of the gloom and into the sunshine for good. But it was like an invisible force, too menacing for her to overcome, held her back.

"Is there any hope for me?" Elizabeth repeatedly asked herself. And, too often, the answer echoing back was, "No." But the fact that Elizabeth still asked the question meant she hadn't given up all hope. Despite how bleak Elizabeth's world had become, there was still hope. There was still time to escape and eventually thrive. But one thing was for sure. She was ready to take action.

The Shark Tale Alternative

*Content that is italicized is repeated from the Fairy Tale version

Elizabeth, a mild-mannered young woman, spent her days working at the local medical school as an administrative assistant. She was satisfied within her job. Serving others suited her well. Sensitive and empathic, she felt a sense of purpose in helping those in her life.

As a young girl, Elizabeth unknowingly became a people-pleaser, because that was the only time she received positive attention from her mother. Her father was around, but he kept his physical and emotional distance, a coping mechanism to keep the peace with his wife. In Elizabeth's youngest years, it seemed that no matter how he interacted with his sweet girl, it was always wrong. He found himself constantly scolded by his wife for how he played with Elizabeth, how he talked to her, how he handled her misbehavior, how he fed her, and so on. Neither Elizabeth's mother nor father had any idea how their choices were shaping their daughter until one day, Elizabeth's father decided he no longer wanted to be afraid of his wife. He read some self-help relationship and parenting books and even went to see a counselor for a few sessions. From those resources, he learned what a healthy relationship with his daughter would look like. He also learned how to set boundaries with his wife in order to enable himself to build that relationship with Elizabeth. Over time, Elizabeth learned that she didn't need to try to please others as a means to gain their attention. And even though her mother didn't change much, the relationship Elizabeth had with her father laid the foundation for a strong sense of her own self-worth.

Each fall, the medical school ushered in a new batch of eager students, ready to take on the world. Elizabeth had worked there for a few years, well acquainted with the staff and students. This particular fall though, she caught the attention of one of the new students. He was tall and mildly handsome, but what he lacked in attractiveness, he made up for in charm. Charisma oozed from his pores. He was intelligent and clever, and whenever he spoke, everyone seemed to listen.

Elizabeth was eating her lunch on a bench outside under one of the many trees on campus when Mark walked by. He stopped, his own lunch in hand, asked if he could sit with her, and introduced himself. Elizabeth assumed he had mistaken her for another medical student and quickly tried to clear up the confusion. However, Mark was quick to point out that he knew exactly who she was and that he had noticed her in the nearby building shortly after orientation. Elizabeth was flattered. The rest of their lunchtime flew by, the conversation flowing smoothly and without the slightest hint of awkwardness. When they finished their sandwiches, Mark walked Elizabeth back to her desk and asked if he could see her again that evening. Elizabeth, without any hesitation, agreed and told Mark when she would be done for the day. He promised to meet her back at her desk at that time.

Four hours later, Elizabeth packed up her belongings, excited for what the evening promised. Five minutes later, no Mark. She found some extra work and kept herself busy for the next thirty minutes, just in case one of his classes ran late. When there was still no Mark, she decided to leave and go home. Disappointed and sad, she ate alone in her apartment that evening.

The next morning, Elizabeth made her way from the parking garage to her desk as she did every day. There was no sign of Mark all day, which was somewhat disappointing since she had hoped to receive an explanation for why he stood her up after their fantastic lunch together. *As the work day ended, she packed up her belongings once again*, this time planning to stop by the grocery store on her way home for some fresh ingredients to make dinner.

Stepping around her desk, a thick voice startled her. "I thought you might need one of these." With instant recognition of the sound, a smile crept to her face, and she looked up. Mark was there, umbrella in hand, ready to escort her to her car. Elizabeth hadn't even realized that it had started pouring rain outside. Telling herself that she was only relieved to have been provided shelter from the downpour, she still knew it was a lie. If Mark had shown up empty-handed, she would have been happy to be drenched walking alongside him. It didn't hurt though, to feel like he had come to her rescue with something as simple as an umbrella.

As they walked through the rain, Mark made his excuses for standing her up the night before, explaining that he had been in the middle of a study group and lost track of time. Elizabeth realized at that moment that, despite her attraction to Mark, he would never be the type of man with whom she knew she wanted to spend her life. She wanted a man who would show up for her when he said he would, respect her enough to value her time, and be so excited to see her that he could never lose track of time leading up to their first date.

As the two approached the parking garage, Mark asked if she would like to go to dinner. Taking a moment to ponder her wording, Elizabeth kindly looked at him and said, "Thank you, Mark, for sharing your umbrella with me this evening and for the lovely time during lunch yesterday, but I am going to have to decline your invitation to dinner. I deserve someone who values me, and I don't want to waste either of our time when I already know that this won't work out." Elizabeth walked away and with a parting glance said, "See you around." Noting the dumbfounded look on Mark's face, Elizabeth smiled as she turned back around, proud of herself for trusting her instincts and valuing herself enough to walk away. No matter how strongly attracted to him she found herself, it would never be worth the portion of her soul she would be sacrificing to be with him.

ACKNOWLEDGMENTS

To my husband: Thank you, my love, for being my greatest supporter and cheerleader, and for the countless hours you allowed me to bounce ideas off of you and talk your ear off about everything in this book. Most of all, thank you for inspiring me to actually write *Swimming with Sharks*.

To my kids: You probably know more about pathological narcissism than nearly every other teenager in the world. Hopefully I didn't give you any unforeseen complexes! If I did though, just remember to keep choosing love over fear!

To each of you in my Coastal Light Counseling family: You're carrying on what I built and making it even more beautiful. Thank you for helping me to share the light of love and acceptance with the world!

To my dearest friends: You know who you are. Thank you for loving me and supporting me along this crazy journey. You've been the comic relief in the movie of my life.

To my mother-in-law: You've made me feel loved from the moment I showed up on your doorstep. Thank you for always being there for me.

To Dr. Ramani Durvasula: Thank you for being the greatest source of information on narcissistic abuse early in my career. Your pioneering work in this field has educated and saved so many, and you are an inspiration to those of us doing this clinical work as well. Also, thank you for responding to my persistent emails asking you to write the foreword. I'm so grateful for the time you took out of your incredibly busy life to support me and this work of love.

To my amazing publishing team at BookLogix: You were the first in the publishing industry to read enough of my book to believe in it. Your praise and support made this finally feel like a reality. You instantly understood me, my idiosyncrasies, and that every choice I make is done with intentionality. Without that, this process might have been arduous and unenjoyable. Instead, you made this one of the greatest experiences I could have asked for. Thank you for not trying to get me to change "theirself" to "themselves." Your help, support, and kind words of praise were so meaningful to me. The graphic design prowess and process was also impeccable. You took my ideas and brought them to life. Thank you for being so patient with me and all of my revision requests. To everyone else behind the scenes, you are greatly appreciated!

ABOUT THE
AUTHOR

A s a psychotherapist and
Licensed Professional
Counselor, Alena Scigliano is
one of very few formally
trained mental health professionals who specializes in
narcissistic abuse. In her private group practice, she provides loving and compassionate
psychotherapy to those who are
searching for healing from relationships
with pathologically narcissistic partners, family members, friends,
coworkers, bosses, pastors, and others. In addition, she supports
other mental health professionals and organizations through narcissistic abuse education, training, and consultation.

Alena's personal mission is to inspire others to live with love, joy,
compassion, and kindness by empowering them to choose love
over fear in every facet of their life. As the founder and CEO of a
multistate group practice, she has built a team of psychotherapists
who are dedicated to improving the lives of hundreds of people

every month. Passionate about innovating the business of counseling, Alena offered teletherapy long before COVID, and has developed innovative forms of therapy such as "Beach & Talk Therapy" and "Indoor Walk & Talk Therapy." Alena also provides consultation to other group practice owners in order to help them improve the systems and processes operating their businesses.

Alena's mental health career was inspired by the powerful changes her own counseling journey made in her life. Therapy helped her learn that even though she and her parents shared a loving relationship, she didn't have the power to stop their alcohol abuse. In addition, it helped her let go of a lifetime of learned fear and anxiety in order to raise her own children in a much healthier environment based on love, joy, and patience. Alena enjoys sharing the difference that unschooling (an unstructured and self-directed type of homeschooling) made in her children's education and their journeys to discovering their individual selves. She passionately advocates for allowing children to hold onto their innate love of learning by embracing their individual learning styles and believes that we succeed as parents if our children know *how* to learn, grow up feeling *loved* and *accepted*, and know how to *love, accept,* and show *compassion* toward *theirselves* and *others*.

COMPANION BOOKS
BY ALENA

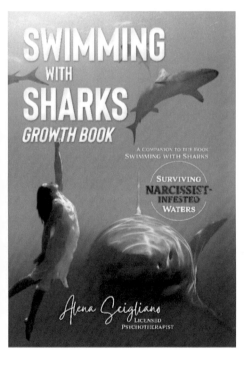

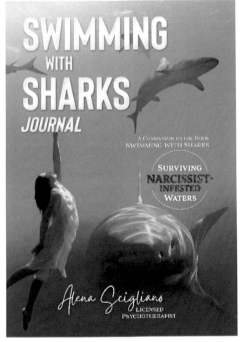